Grace Note
Publications

This Edition of *The Eric R. Cregeen Fieldwork Journals* is published thanks to the
support of **Grace Notes Scotland,** a Scottish Charity
dedicated to identifying and handing on traditions to new generations.

All projects conserve, nurture and promote Scotland's languages and dialects,
traditions and skills, oral history, songs, tunes and stories.
www.gracenotescotand.org

The Eric R. Cregeen Fieldwork Journals Index

Eric R. Cregeen and Lachlan MacLeod, Grimsay, North Uist, 1969

The Eric R. Cregeen Fieldwork Journals 1939-1982

Volume 10
Index

*For Irene,
with appreciation,
Margaret Bennett*

Margaret Bennett
Editor

Grace Notes Scotland
Grace Note Publications

Original Journals © The Estate of the late E. R. Cregeen
Introduction & Transcriptions © Margaret Bennett, 2019
© Grace Notes Scotland, 2019
© Grace Note Publications, 2019

The Eric R. Cregeen Fieldwork Journals:
Pathways to sustainability of land-use,
language and culture

1939-1982

Volume 10
Index

ISBN: 978-1-907676-99-4

Grace Notes Scotland
Registered Scottish Charity (SC040434)
Dunira, Comrie, PH6 2JZ, Scotland

Project director:
Margaret Bennett, BA (Ed), MA, PhD, DMus (Hon), HRSA
info@gracenotescotland.org
www.gracenotescotland.org

Typeset by Grace Note Publications
in collaboration with Grace Notes Scotland

Grace Note Publications C.I.C.
Grange of Locherlour, Ochtertyre, PH7 4JS
books@gracenotereading.co.uk

British Library Cataloguing-in-Publication Data
A catalogue record for this book is available from the British Library

Supported by

Eric R. Cregeen (1921-1983)

Oral History presents us with a rich and diverse store of source-material ... The recordings we make now will be a powerful aid to future generations living in a much-changed society.

Eric R. Cregeen,

Scottish Oral History Group, 1978

Contents

Introduction 1

Volume 1: Journals 1939-1949 3

Volume 2: Journals 1949-1957 6

Volume 3: Journals 1955-1959 10

Volume 4: Journals 1959-1968 15

Volume 5: Journals 1969-1972 21

Volume 6: Journals 1973-1974 28

Volume 7: Journals 1974-1978 35

Volume 8: Journals 1975-1976 42

Volume 9: Journals 1977-1982 49

Appendix A: "The Life and Legacy of Eric R. Cregeen" 57

Appendix B: Publications by Eric R. Cregeen 63

Appendix C: Publications about and including the work of Eric R. Cregeen 65

Acknowledgements 67

INTRODUCTION

This index has been compiled as a follow-up to a Grace Note Scotland project to digitise, transcribe and print the fieldwork journals of Eric Radcliffe Cregeen (1921–83). The journals, written between 1939 and 1982, contain a record of Cregeen's ideas, travels, and fieldwork carried out in the Isle of Man, Ireland, and the West Highlands of Scotland. They include notes on local culture; social history; features of landscape and archaeology; development of research methods; and accounts of travels and visits he made in his quest to document the way of life and traditions of people he saw, met, sought out, visited, and/or interviewed.

Eric R. Cregeen is now regarded internationally as one of the most influential oral historians of the 20th century. Meticulous in his methodology, he anticipated using his journals for further research and a series of publications, but, sadly, that was not to be. Eric died in 1983, and since that time, as custodian of the journals, Mrs Lily Cregeen has hoped that her husband's fieldwork would be of use in further research. In 2016, she invited me to visit her, read Eric's journals and, as a fellow folklorist, oral historian and former lecturer at the University of Edinburgh's School of Scottish Studies, share my ideas on how they might be conserved and used in further research. It was immediately apparent that, to do justice to the forty years of fieldwork, this was not a 'retirement project' or a 'one-person-task'; it would require a team of dedicated helpers. Thus began an 18-month project: "The Cregeen Journals: Sustainability, Land-use, Language and Culture". With funding from Heritage Lottery Fund, Grimsay Community Association and Grace Note Publications, over 4,000 pages were digitised and transcribed by an invaluable team of helpers, and finally typeset, printed and bound in nine volumes by Grace Note Publications.

This additional volume, the index, is to support researchers wishing to access the journals. It is set out in nine sections, with each journal (labelled by year) having its own index. The subject entries are wide-ranging across topics and disciplines, as well as geographic areas. The extent and the detail included reflect Eric Cregeen's training, which began while he was a student volunteer in the Manx Museum. Though he was later to develop his methodology for recording oral history, he owed his early discipline to the training at the Manx Museum, where instructions to volunteers were based on the pioneering work of the Irish Folklore Commission, particularly that of Seán Ó Súilleabháin. His *Handbook of Irish Folklore* (Dublin, 1942) has become a classic guide for fieldworkers and continues to be regarded internationally as the 'folklorist's bible'. Though there have been great advances in technology, training today still emphasises the importance of using the best available equipment to record voices for future generations. To this end, in 1948 the volunteers were given 'hands-on' fieldwork training from Kevin Danaher of the Irish Folklore Commission, who, (at the urgent request of Irish Taeshoch, Eamon de Valera), was sent to the Isle of Man to record Manx speakers. Eric was among the trainees who learned the skill of cutting the laminate disc recordings that would eventually inspire the revival of the Manx language and save it from extinction. Seventy years on, Cregeen's fieldwork, like that of Scotland's Calum Maclean, bears the hallmark of the rigorous training of the Irish Folklore Commission.

A more detailed biographical essay about Eric R. Cregeen introduces each volume, and for those who wish to access information about his life and legacy it is reprinted at the end of this one [see Appendix A]. Despite widespread regret that Cregeen did not live long enough to complete the publications he had planned, he nevertheless produced a remarkable number of books and articles [see Appendix B]. Since his death, other publications of his work have appeared, as well as some that draw from his fieldwork [see Appendix C].

There are several references to reel-to-reel tape recordings in the fieldwork notes and index, and it is evident that Cregeen added the accession numbers after they had been deposited in the School of Scottish Studies Archive. The form of reference is standard and fits with the format used in that archive; for example, SA1976/47, denotes the year filed in the Sound Archives, followed by the number in a sequence of tapes deposited in that year. A selection of the recordings can be consulted via the website Tobar and Dualchais/ Kist o Riches.

To date, 2019, the 9 volumes of the Cregeen Journals may be consulted via several libraries and other centres, including:

> Bodleian Libraries of the University of Oxford
>
> Cambridge University Library
>
> Harvard Library, Cambridge MA
>
> Manx National Heritage Library & Archive
>
> Department of Folklore, Memorial University of Newfoundland, St John's, NL
>
> The Library of Trinity College, Dublin
>
> The National Library of Scotland
>
> The National Library of Wales
>
> The University of Edinburgh Library (Special Collections)
>
> The University of Glasgow Library
>
> The University of Newcastle Library
>
> The Grimsay Community Association, North Uist
>
> The Scottish Crofting Federation, Kyle of Lochalsh
>
> Tiree's Historical Centre, An Iodhlann, Isle of Tiree

It is hoped that Eric R. Cregeen's work will eventually be accessible online, via the University of Glasgow's digital project to support Scottish Gaelic (DASG), and via a website planned by the School of Scottish and Celtic Studies at the University of Edinburgh. Meanwhile, encouraged by the interest already shown in the Cregeen Journals, it is hoped that this index will stimulate further research and lead to many more publications.

Margaret Bennett, 2019

INDEX VOLUME 1
1939-1949

B

Blacksmith *104, 243, 247, 284*

C

Ceilidh *194*
Simon Crowe *248*

D

Digital Archive of Scottish Gaelic (DASG) *4*
Diagrams (see also Sketches) *217, 219, 259, 30–08, 310*
Donegal Tweed *195*

E

Eric's family
    Aunt Alice *203*
    Lily Cregeen *3, 5*
    Thomas Cregeen *263*
    Gill *104, 293*
    Grandad - Radcliffe *98–105, 111, 142, 272*
    Kitty Quane *105*
    Mrs Quane *104*
    Allen Radcliffe *243*
    Auntie Annie *100, 101, 142, 145*
    Aunt Lily Radcliffe *99*
    Radcliffe Genealogy *1, 104, 113–14, 141, 205, 209, 243*
    Betsy Shand *104*
    Sheila Cregeen *136, 156ff*.

F

Farms, Farming
    Ballagayle *289*
    Cows *294*
    Cronk Cornan *219*
    Crops (see Food)

Fisheries *309*
Fishermen, sayings *3, 98, 105, 140*
Folklife Surveys *1, 2, 313*
Food
    Oats *172*
    Porridge *160*
    Potatoes *143, 172, 309, 310*
    Rye *172*

G

Gaelic *2, 4, 103, 167, 171, 188, 192–93, 195, 215*

I

Informants
    Lord Asbourne *102*
    Katie Brown *272*
    T. E. Brown *243*
    Tommy Cashia *102*
    Cesar Cashin *98–99, 102–03, 109–12*
    Ewan Christian *103, 208*
    Miss Coisley *136*
    Mrs Connell *180*
    Arthur Corteen *284, 289–99, 304*
    Charlie Craine *104*
    Neddie Crowe *290*
    William Cubbon *261, 266, 312*
    Tom Dodd *103, 113*
    John Gaune *262*
    Andrew Joughin *243, 245–48, 306*
    John Thom Kaighin *244, 261*
    Arthur Karran *261*
    Mrs. Keggan *263, 264*
    Cecil Kelly *309, 311–12*
    Frank Kelly *137, 208*
    Mrs Kneale *106, 110, 114*
    John Kreen *244, 261–62, 299*
    Ned Maddrell *208, 262*
    Tommy Madrell *97*
    Ramsey Moore *264–65*
    Murrg *174*

Charlie Palmer *111, 147, 203*
Perric *99*
Quilliam *98*
Leslie Quirk *112, 201*
John Sayle *97*
T.W. Stowell *259–260*
Philly The Desert *266*
Wm. Thwaites *116*
Tom Todd *112–113*
Will Waid *205, 244*

Irish Folklore Commission *1, 2*

M

Manx *viii, 1, 2, 98, 100, 102–04, 106, 108–11, 115–16, 120, 13–38, 140–42, 146–47, 149, 151, 156–57, 162, 172, 192–93, 195, 200–04, 207–08, 211–12, 215, 243–45, 248, 262, 272, 288, 293, 299, 301, 306*
    Manx Bible *146, 201, 248*
    Manx Museum *viii, 2, 137, 141, 156, 211, 212, 306*
    Old Manx people *108*

Musician
    William Cubbon (fiddlers) *261, 266, 312*

O

Old sayings *102*

P

Place-names
    Aran Islands *171–73*
    Ballanayre *201, 203–04, 209*
    Ballaugh *145–46, 204, 206, 209, 261*
    Ballygarrett *106*
    Clifton *169, 170*
    Connemara *164, 167, 169, 171*
    Cork *179, 185, 187–88, 190–91, 197*
    Cronk Brae *263*
    Douglas *viii, 7, 99–100, 102–03, 110, 136–37, 140–42, 147–48, 201, 203, 208, 243, 284–85, 293, 304, 312*
    Dublin *2, 103ff.*
    Dun Aengus *172–73*
    Dun Laoghaire *155, 182*
    Galway *162ff.*
    Glendalough *158–59, 178*
    Glendalough Lake *178*
    Glengarriff *185, 192–93, 196*
    Glen Helen *102*
    Glen Maye *99*
    Glen Rushen *104*
    Inishmore *172*
    Isle of Man *viii, 1–4, 7, 8, 102, 153, 161, 211*
    Killarney *183, 192*
    Kilmurvey *172*
    Kilronan *172*
    Limerick *178, 194, 198*
    Macclesfield *182, 189*
    Oughterard *167–69, 176*
    Patrick Glen *104*
    Peel *viii, 1, 7, 97, 99, 102, 111, 135–37, 139–41, 144, 146–48, 201, 203–04, 206, 208–09, 243, 245, 271, 293–95*
    Port Erin *139–40, 262–64*
    Poul-Gorm *189*
    Ringway *200*
    Tour of Ireland *viii, 153*
    Tynewald *102, 103, 113*
    Weatherglass, Peel *97*
    West Highlands *3, 4, 6*
    Wicklow county *158*

R

Ration coal *184*

S

Sketches (see also Diagrams) *268–71*
Stone-walling *289*
    Arthur Corteen *284, 289, 299, 304*
    Neddie Crowe *290*
Superstitious beliefs
    Charms *107, 108*

Evil eye *116*
Fairies *116, 261, 266*
Fairy Tune *267*
Pishagyn *107*
Superstitions *107, 108*
Witchcraft *107*

T

Thatched houses *146, 165–66, 169, 172, 219, 293, 295, 309*
Traditional Customs
    Burning the Buitch *107*
    Chruinnaght *111*
    Crosh-Keira *107*
    Good Friday *102, 107, 184*
    Hop-Naa *102*
    Hunting of the "Wran" *107*
    Hunting the wren *102*
    Limpets in Good Friday *102*
    Old Christmas *107*
    Old St. Bride's Day *111*
    Periwinkles in Good Friday *102*
    Shenu Laa'e Brishay *111*
    The White Boys *102*
    Tynewald Day *102*
Trinity College *156*

W

Whisky *3, 174*
Whisky-dealer *174*
Writers
    Margaret Bennett *v, vi, 3, 5, 6*
    Willie Douglas *100*
    Martin MacGregor *3*
    Pat Mullen *172*
    Sean O-Casey *157*
    Seán Ó Súilleabháin *2*
    T. C. Smout *3*

INDEX VOLUME 2
1949-1957

A

Amusements *40*
Animals
    Cows *15, 40–1, 73, 81, 161, 293*
    Horses *3, 81, 114–15, 123–24, 127, 244, 251, 292, 298*
    Pigs *105*
    Sheep *295*
    Tram-horses *81*

B

Beer *162*
Boat-Building *179*
    Buildings
        Ballamodha Chapel *89*
        Braddan Churchyard *63*
        Fort *32, 33, 97, 371*
        Home at West Berk *142*
        Keeill *14, 17–22, 26, 120, 126*
        Kerrookeeil Chapel *119*
        Mill *18, 27, 75, 95–96, 102, 105, 117, 129, 140, 159, 252–53, 297–98*
        Sartfell cottage *18*
        Turf-house *139, 239*

C

Carranes *162*
Cregeen's Dictionary *72*
Crofters *3*
Crofts *25, 47, 81, 129, 174, 257, 295*
    Crofter-Firshermen *92, 295–96, 310–11*
    Crofter-Miners *81, 92*
Crops (see also Food)
    Harvest & Corn *49*
    Oat-meal & Barley-meal *293*

D

Digital Archive of Scottish Gaelic (DASG) *4*
Diagrams *35, 135, 144–56, 298, 314, 327–29, 331–50, 366–75, 378*

E

Emigration *258*
Eric's family
    Cregeen family *307*
    Lily Cregeen *3, 5*
    Kirsty *5*
    Patrick Baptisms *218*
    Patrick Marriages *218, 222–24, 227*
    Radcliffe Baptismal Records *187*
    Radcliffe Family *189*
    Radcliffe Genealogy *1*
    Radcliffes in German *201*
    Thomas Radcliffe *188, 194–96, 215, 219, 223–24*
    William Radcliffe *35–36, 49, 118, 159, 188ff.*
    Selwyn Letter *289, 385*

F

Fairies (see Supernatural)
Farms/Farming *364, 368*
    Eairy ny Seire *11*
    Farmer's Questionnaire *249*
    Glen Rushen *21, 188, 295, 307–08, 363–67*
    Grazing Rights *255*
    Harvest-Field *50*
    Kerrookeeill *36, 43, 60–61, 75–6, 86–9, 119-21, 314*
    Lazy-Beds *50*
    Nab Farm *28, 32*
    Narey *11*
    Neairey *18-22, 28*
    Neairy *13*
    Sartfell *18, 23*

Southampton Farm *364, 368*
St. John's *21, 162, 291, 363*
The Raggy *43*
Tosaby *21*
Virginia *15, 17, 98*
Farm Implements
Ploughs *241*
Sickles *160*
Seed-sowing implements *242*
Turf spades *240*
Tractor *123, 124*
Fishing *173–78*
Boat-Building *179*
Folklife Surveys *2*
Food (see also Crops)
Boats, Diet *137*
Butter-making *111–12, 161*
Corn *50, 75, 95, 105, 123–24, 129, 135, 160, 244, 250–51*
Oatmeal *20, 138, 249, 293*

G

Gaelic *2, 4, 52, 58, 59, 165, 312, 325, 380*

H

Health
Depression (Smull) *34, 138*
Silicosis *81*

I

Informants
Matthew Arnold *37*
Harry Boyde *30–1, 51–5, 68,–9*
Richard Cain *160*
Archie Campbell *5*
Annie Cannell *49*
Mr. Clague *19, 20, 297–99*
Mrs. Colvin *38*
John Corlett *291*
Jotty Corlett *85, 113, 184*
Keith Corlett *125, 133–34, 190–91*
Cowley *97, 123, 126–32, 159, 184, 209*
William Cubbon *35, 118, 301, 373*
Willie Dodd *179*
Mrs. Faragher *368*
William Faragher *159*
Bert Garrett *36–7, 43–8, 60, 65, 72–86, 105, 111–19, 184,*
John Garrett *140, 295, 296*
John Gaune *173, 303*
Mrs. Gill *301, 363, 364, 365*
John Thom Kaighier *276*
Arthur Kervin *114, 115, 116*
John Kinvig *37, 73, 96*
Mrs. Kinvig *168, 171, 291-95*
Tom Leece *57*
Ned Maddrell *165, 171, 317-19*
Richard Moore *376*
Walter Moore *69, 71*
William Moore *36, 49, 61, 66, 114, 123*
Miss Quayle *157*
Harry Sagle *46*
John Scarffe *87, 96, 101, 108, 110*
Billy Taggart *48, 72*
Tom Taggart *86–7, 121–22*
Mrs. Teare *136, 363*
Tommy Watson *62*
Irish Folklore Commission *1, 2*

L

Local Patriotism *98*
Cess on Land (Local tax) *117*
Lowlander *128*

M

Manx *29-30, 38, 44, 51-52, 56–59, 64, 78, 83, 87, 93, 99, 101–04, 106, 129, 138–39, 165, 168–71, 174, 176, 179, 185, 237ff.*
Chiollagh *15*
Manx lecture 1971 *303*
Manx Phrases *7, 30, 52, 68*

Manx Museum *7*
    Bishop Phillips Prayer Book *301*
    Mr Curphey *264*
Manx Place-Names *58, 59*
Basil Megaw *2*
Medical, cures and charms *83–85, 113–14, 136*
Mines
    Foxdale mines *43, 80–81, 90–93*
    Foxdale Slate Quarries *82*

N

National Museum of Ireland *331*

P

Peg-leg Caley *42*
Place-names
    America *43, 80, 92, 307, 389*
    Baldwin *9–13, 18–19, 28, 95, 108, 110*
    Ballacreeich *95*
    Ballafreer *14*
    Ballagawne *97*
    Ballaharry *28–33*
    Ballamodha *60ff.*
    Ballaquine *10, 20*
    Ballavagher *36, 44, 66, 114*
    Beary Mountain *18, 26*
    Camlurk *14*
    Castletown *50ff. 140, 184*
    Creg *10–12, 18, 129*
    Dalby *21, 80, 308, 310, 311*
    Douglas *24, 38, 39ff. 305, 319, 363*
    Druidale *125–29*
    Eairy Cushlin *21*
    German *189ff.*
    Glen Rushen *21, 188, 295, 307–08, 363–67*
    Isle of Man *7, 128, 136, 173, 187, 289, 303, 318*
    Kerroomooar *36, 73, 90, 114, 120, 139, 140, 184, 295, 314–16*
    Kerroo Mooar *47, 57*
    Lhergy Ruy *12*
    Little London *18, 25*
    Niarbyl *94, 324*
    Peel *80, 93, 133–34, 173–75, 179, 185, 189, 190–96, 211, 217, 235–36, 306ff.*
    Rhenass *18, 25*
    Strang *14, 18, 96, 108, 379*
Plants
    Red Bracken *25*
Public House *77*

S

School of Scottish Studies Archives
    Recorded *1, 3, 6*
Smith
    Smith's Questionnaire *238, 239*
Supernatural
    Fairy-Doctor *114, 136*
    Fairy Music *108–10*
    Fairy-woman *136, 363*
Superstitious beliefs
    Boats-Superstitions *137*
    Charms *83–85, 113–14, 136*
    Death-Signs *114–16*
    Fishing Supernatural *178*
    Omens *111*
    Witchcraft *111–13*

T

Tea *23–24, 42, 118, 314*
Thatched Houses *47, 72, 157, 252, 315, 380*
Traditional Customs
    Candlemas Saying *65*
    Christmas *56*
    Clish (lucky stone) *291*
    Douglas Fair *40*
    Good Friday *94*
    Hollantide *39, 83*
    Mheillea *49*
    Oie'll Verree *86*

Tynwald Day *39*
Xmas *38, 39, 67*

W

Whalliag *47*
Whisky *42*
Writers
    Margaret Bennett *3, 5, 6*
    Martin MacGregor *3*
    Seán Ó Súilleabháin *2*
    T. C. Smout *3*

INDEX VOLUME 3
1955-1959

A

Archaeological Sites
    Blarbuie rings *167*
    Cairn Port Donan *79*
    Crachan *248*
    Cup-marked Stone *33, 35*
    Dun Hiader *95*
    Dun Nosebridge *305, 308*
    Dun Vaul Beg *110–13*
    Dun Vaul Mor *110–11*
    Eaglais Tobair *317*
    Fossilised tree in Mull *248*
    Leim *76*
    Moss Stone Circle *94*
    Mull Antiquities *72*
    Sandhills at Ruaig *97*
    Standing Stone near Dumhoon *247*
    Tomb Cragabus Islay *154*

B

Barley straws *188*
Bishop Carswell *43*
Buildings
    Black house *81–84, 201*
    Castle Sween *18*
    Chapel Kilmahe *160*
    Keill Chapel *70*
    Kirkapoll Churches *104*
    Kitchen Midden *114*
    Lewis Black House *197*
    Long houses *294*
    Temple Patrick *96*

C

Carpet factory *19*
Clearances, see Evictions *90, 237, 294*
    Cuichaoiram *52*
    Killerin *165*

Clothing & footwear *44*
Crofter-Fishermen *341*
Crofts *19, 71, 92, 129, 165, 285, 344-45*

D

Digital Archive of Scottish Gaelic (DASG) *4*
Diagrams (see also Sketches) *4, 17, 26–31, 36, 69, 73, 77–78, 80–81, 86, 89, 91, 96, 99, 100–07, 132, 136–38, 145, 147, 149, 151, 154, 160, 162–63, 165–70, 172*
Droving *40, 119, 156*
    Auchindrain *58, 115–17, 124–25, 173, 248*
    Mr. Benny *127*
    Brenachoillie *129*
    Hugh Cameron *125*
    Drove-road *128, 298*
    Drovers *320, 324*
    Falkirk (Tryst) *65, 120, 123–24, 128, 157, 210, 293, 324*
    Glen Douglas *119, 122, 129–30*
    Inverbeg Inn *120–22, 126*
    Robert Kerr *120–22*
    Kilmichael Tryst *327*
    Mr. Macfarlane *123*
    Dougall MacDougall *40—65, 67, 116, 127*
    Dugald MacDougall *128, 158, 292, 321*
    Dugald MacIntyre *119, 128, 210*
    Mr. McFarlane *124, 127, 274–75*
    Merkins' Farm *127*
    Munro's house at Auchengaul, *292*
    Perthshire *121*
    Mr Robertson *120*
    Gilbert Stevenson *158*
    Stronafyne *123, 125–27, 130*
Duke of Argyll *13, 22, 87, 165, 333*

E

Eric's family
    Lily Cregeen *3, 5, 94, 115, 119, 127, 295, 305, 342*

Evictions, see Clearances
    Battle of Arichonan *53*

F

Famine Road *318*
Farms, Farming
    Achnaba farms *293*
    Auchentiobairt *22*
    Auchnagaul *57, 61, 71*
    Caora fhuadainn *192*
    Creag a' Gat *15*
    Lazy-bed *88, 338, 344*
    Merkins Farm *127*
    Questions Cattle *66, 227*
    Seaweed *57, 59, 89, 139*
    Smearing tar on sheep *189*
    Stronafyne Farm *123*
    Tiroran Farm *294*
Farm Implements
    Cas-chrom *14, 15, 188,*
    Ditching Spade *319*
    Flail *131, 143, 146, 156, 172, 196, 242, 281, 316–17*
    Horse-hair ropes *287*
    Peat spade *141*
    Thrashing machine *146–48, 155, 156*
Fishermen, Sailors & Boats
    Boats & fishing *182*
    Drifters *215, 330*
    Fifie *182–83, 185*
    Fishing *viii, 46, 60, 133–34, 138, 175, 182–84, 201, 209, 211–13, 227, 230–31, 233, 237–38, 292–93, 322ff.*
    Herring *215, 230–31, 235, 329, 356–59*
    Tom Jackson *235, 342*
    Salmon spear, *136*
    Shares in the boats *357, 371*
    Skaff *185*
    Tarbert Fishing *350*
    Zulu *182, 183, 185*

Folklorists
    Kevin Danaher *2*
    Hamish Henderson *211, 289*
    Calum MacLean *296, 321*
Folklife Surveys *2*

G

Gaelic *viii, 2, 4, 12, 20, 39, 48, 56–57, 60, 65, 131, 135, 140, 157, 159–80, 213, 219, 223, 230, 234, 238, 242, 275–76, 285, 291, 296, 321, 324, 356, 359, 361, 367, 377–78, 388*
Glossary Gaelic words *180*

I

Informants
    Archie Campbell *5*
    Roderick Campbell *177–203*
    Miss Daisy Craig *143*
    Duncan Currie *293*
    Jean Currie *146*
    Dugal Dall *24*
    Folklore Informants, 1957 *209*
    Alistair Fraser *64*
    Mr Gordon *213, 313*
    Angus Henderson *72, 75, 136, 141, 276, 278, 285, 325, 338*
    Mary Henderson *140–41*
    Mr Hodkinson *298, 299, 300*
    Duncan Hunter *133*
    John Johnson *168, 213, 230–33*
    Mrs Livinstone *295–96*
    MacAlpine *213, 230–32, 235, 350*
    Mr J. MacArthur *341*
    Duncan MacColl *13, 20, 22, 63, 210, 292, 341*
    Mr Hamish MacCuaig *146*
    Alistair MacDonald *54*
    Lachie Macdonald *109*
    Dougall MacDougall *41, 43, 59, 65, 67, 116, 127*

Dugald MacDougall *128, 158, 292, 321*
Duncan MacDougall *155*
Mr. MacDougall, junr *60*
Mrs Ann MacDougall *129*
Kenneth MacFarlane *76, 213, 274, 328, 346, 380*
Davy MacFarlane *213, 328, 380*
Donald MacFarlane *275*
Kenneth MacFarlane *74, 76, 344, 346*
Mr MacInnes *297*
James Mackintosh *324, 326, 336, 360, 362–73*
Calum MacLean *296, 321*
Donald MacLean *321*
Mr MacLellan *322*
Alistair MacLeod *293*
MacNab *335*
John MacPhee *211, 289*
Mrs MacPhee *211, 288–91*
Angus MacTaggart *33*
Dougall MacTaggart *33, 39*
McCallum *337*
Mr D. McColl *19*
Hamish McCuay *145*
Mr. Mckechnan *155*
Duncan McKeith *241*
Johnny McLachlan *378*
Iain Mor Creag *15*
Mr MacAuley *304*
John O'Hara *134*
Skye informants *214*
Dr Smith *306–19*
Mrs Strachan, Tarbert *216*
Tiree Informants *214*
Miss Williamson *314*
Mr Wilson *84, 94, 111*
Irish Folklore Commission *1, 2*

K

Knapdale Recollections *48-49*

M

Neil MacGilvray *279*
MacMillans of Knapdale *46*
Maps *24, 248, 304, 318*
Mills *45, 237, 283*

P

Peat *15–21, 57, 141, 202, 276, 283, 286, 320, 345*
Peat spade *141*
Place-names
    Ardnacross *229*
    Auchantiobairt *13*
    Auchendrain *61, 63, 165, 212*
    Auchengaul *292*
    Auchnacraig *77*
    Auchnagaul *57, 61, 71*
    Auchnangaul *20, 22, 123, 125*
    Balemartin *82, 109, 214*
    Balephuill Bay *94*
    Ballinoe *82, 95, 209*
    Barra *88, 92, 209, 211, 291, 346*
    Bowmore *298–300, 321*
    Bridge of Douglas *20*
    Calgary *271-272*
    Campbeltown *134, 212–13, 322, 324, 333ff.*
    Carnasserie *45, 55*
    Carradale *8, 209, 211, 236–37, 240–41, 324–26, 354ff.*
    Cluanary *19, 22–23*
    Crarae *13*
    Craignish *49, 295–96, 375*
    Dervaig *72–76, 274, 278*
    Dun Hiader *95*
    Dun Hianish *89*
    Dun Kenovay *90*
    Dun Mor Vaul *87*
    Fife *240, 354, 371*
    Glen Aros *75*
    Glen Douglas *119, 122, 129–30*

Inveraray *23, 53, 71, 210, 336, 341, 372*
Invershin *143*
Iona *9, 278*
Island of Borrera *9*
Islay *viii, 144, 147, 154–56, 159, 213, 251, 298–99, 306, 308, 313–14, 319, 356, 369*
Kenmore *15, 20–21, 336, 341*
Kilbride *8, 16*
Kilinevair *65, 115–16*
Kilmartin *288, 296–97, 327, 337, 378*
Kilmoluag *85*
Kilmory Knap *8, 33, 39, 209*
Laninne Sgier *273*
Laphroaig *313–14*
Lewis *175, 179, 182, 192–93, 197, 199, 201, 379*
Loch a' Chaoruinn *117*
Loch Awe *115, 125, 211*
Loch Ederline (Gucumgo site) *54*
Loch Fyne *117, 234, 239, 240, 330–31, 336, 341, 350, 354, 357–58, 369, 372*
Loch Teacuis *11*
Mallaig *331*
Minard *41, 43, 57, 60, 67, 210, 212, 292, 326, 335, 341, 372*
Mull *7, 9, 72, 136, 141–42, 205, 212, 225, 248, 251, 277, 278, 287, 296, 346*
Pennymore *13*
Poltalloch *41, 43, 51–52, 128, 130, 378*
Rahoy *11*
Ruaig *97*
Scarinish *82, 89, 288, 291*
Stenndrum *19*
Tarbert *67, 126, 130, 209, 210, 212–13, 216, 230–31, 234–35, 240, 326, 328, 332–33, 343, 350–51, 362*
Tiree *7, 80–84, 89, 94, 110, 140–41, 156, 205, 209, 211, 214, 251, 281, 288, 291, 321, 345–46*

Tobermory *9, 72, 76, 136, 143, 212, 225, 274, 276, 278, 284–85, 296, 338, 344–46*
Torrisdale *326, 352, 359, 360, 363, 365*
Ulva *278, 344*
West Argyll *viii, 7*

R

Railway *225, 331*
Religion
    Fenced communion tables *318*

S

School of Scottish Studies Archives
    Recorded *1, 3, 6*
Shepherd's plaid *45*
Shieling *299, 315, 379*
Sketches (see also Diagrams) *282, 285, 289, 303, 308, 317, 320*
Smith *39, 139, 276, 278, 286*
    Blacksmith *68, 75*
    Sword-maker *300*
Song, singing
    Miss Dixon *143*
    Lullabies *200*
    Psalm *200–01*
    Waulking Songs *187*
Spinning and Weaving *190*
Stone dykes *148, 149*
Storytelling, Story
    Stories from Mull *9*
    Story from Mrs Livingstone *295*
    Story of Niall *280*
    Story of the Minister of Glass *315*
    story of the pig *92*
    Story of *three fichid burraidhean* *297*
Sun-dial *352*
Supernatural
    Fairy music *39*
Superstitious beliefs
    Evil eye *210, 238*

Fishermen supertitions *60, 232, 322,*
326, 330–34, 341, 350, 353, 356, 358,
360, 368
Rowan *62*
White whale *341*
Witchcraft *58*

T

Traditional Customs
Coffin-Rest *65*
Harvest Maiden *295–97*
Oatmeal to cure cattle *64*
Prohibition at sea *238*
Thatched houses *48, 81–84, 145, 149, 165,*
193, 197, 211, 284, 288, 290, 345
Barley stalk for thaching *188*

W

Waulking cloth *191*
Wells
Holy Well *13*
Priest's Well *73*
Whisky *3, 47, 313, 316, 325*
Distillery *313, 314*
Glenlivet *314*
Writers
Margaret Bennett *3, 5, 6*
Martin MacGregor *3*
Seán Ó Súilleabháin *2*
T. C. Smout *3*

INDEX VOLUME 4
1959-1968

A

Animals, birds
    Eagle *234*
    Horses 143
    Wild Boar *234*
Archaeological Sites
    Cairn at Ardnacross *26*
    Cairn at Kilninian *26*
    Cup-and-Ring Marked Stone *38*
    Dug-out canoe *36*
    Dun Ara *9, 17, 26*
    Dun Ban *9, 13, 25, 27*
    Dun Eiphin *15*
    Dun Hynish *60*
    Standing Stone at Strotian Hotel *40*
    Taigh an Duin *14*

B

Baillidh Mòr *331*
Last Balranald: Capt Alexr. MacDonald *271*
Battle of Arichonan *220*
Blacksmith *173, 176, 189, 255*
    Armourers *176*
    Blacksmith & Magic *257*
    Smiths of Ardtonish *230, 286*
Buildings
    Balranald house *266–67, 269, 272, 274*
    Barn *9, 11, 55, 71, 83, 88–89, 110, 115, 352*
    Black houses *348*
    Kilmartin Churchyard *51*
    Kirkapoll House *12*
    Long houses *55–56, 66, 72, 115*
    Minard Castle *9, 10, 57–58*
    Quinish House *16*

C

Clearances (see also Evictions) *201, 259*
    Calgary *251*
    Greaullin *217*
    Killian *351*
    Mull *259*
    Sollas *201*
Crofters *3, 55,* 125, *158, 175, 181, 230, 243, 270–71, 295, 369*
Crofts *43, 202, 275, 278–79, 301–02, 369*
Croig Pier *250*

D

Digital Archive of Scottish Gaelic (DASG) *4*
Diagrams (see also Illustrations & sketchs) *4*
Duke of Argyll *92, 95, 213, 259, 294, 301, 315, 351–52, 355*

E

Eric's lectures
    Cornaigmore School – Tiree *46*
Eric's planning
    Mull & Kintyre *93*
    Research 1959 – MSS & Recordings *96*
Evictions, see also Clearances
    Malcolm MacLaurine *315*
    Patrick Sellar *230, 286*

F

Factors, see also Baillidh Mòr *95, 295, 302, 313–16, 324, 348*
    Malcolm MacLaurine *315*
    Patrick Sellar *230, 286*
Famine *131, 252*
    Famine relief tower: Scolpaig *265*
    Famine Road *252*
    Potato famine *259*
Farms, Farming
    Bent grass *60*
    Canesby Farm *105*
    Grianan Farm *239*
    Joint Tenants *351*
    Kilmichael farm *237*
    Knock Farm *156, 190*

Lazy-beds *44, 48, 55, 73, 165, 275, 276*
Lower Neribolls Farm *119*
Milking *343*
Milling *302*
Potatoes *81, 276–79, 343*
Seaweed *231, 276, 279, 301, 311, 344, 356*
Threshing *71, 110*

Farm Implements
Cas-chrom *165, 275, 276, 277*
Flail *9, 46, 47, 71, 176, 326*
Kilns *9, 44, 47, 48, 115, 117, 118, 305*

Fishermen, Sailors & Boats
Eun Mara *246*
Fisherman and Boat-builder *240*
Shellfish *235*
Trapping fish *236*

Folklife Surveys *2*
Food *81, 335, 343*
Carageen *344*
Crockans *343*

G

Gaelic *2, 4, 9-10, 62, 80, 88-89, 153ff.*,
Maclean genealogy *183, 304, 339*

H

Hunting with dogs *235*

I

Illustrations [see also diagrams & sketches] *12–14, 23, 27, 29, 30–34, 36–37, 41–43, 51, 56, 62, 66, 69, 74–79, 84–85*

Informants
Ardnamruchan Informants *215*
Willie Boyd *201*
Neil Brownlie *177, 203*
Alastair Cameron *230, 286*
Alex Campbell *9, 38*
Archie Campbell *5*
Mary Anne Campbell *171, 327, 338*
Sandy Campbell *157, 160–61, 171, 203, 316*
Jessie Craig *258, 259*
John Dunbar *57*
Winnie Ewing *245, 246*
Professor T. N. George *34-35*
Angus Henderson *95, 164, 189, 246, 249–54, 295*
Informants list: 1968 *153*
Donald Alasdair Johnson *201*
Jura informants *181*
Hector Kennedy (Eachainn Mòr) *172*
Ian Lamont *33*
Lewis Informant *183*
Nicol Logan *139*
Alistair MacArthur *171*
Donald MacArthur *217*
Mrs Macarthur *199*
Atty MacCallum *25, 27*
Eddie MacCallum *350, 357, 360*
Mr MacCallum *142*
Mrs MacCallum *172*
MacCrae from Kirkton *85, 86*
Angus John MacDonald *263*
Calum MacDonald *173, 187, 308*
Donald Angus MacDonald *201*
Donald Eoghain MacDonald *230, 266, 267, 269, 271–74, 281*
Hugh MacDonald *172, 202, 209*
John MacDonald *153, 159, 197, 230, 236, 263–67, 279, 280, 323*
Malcolm MacDonald *307*
Dougald MacDougall *220*
Neil MacDougall *161, 240*
Hughie MacEacheran *176*
K. MacFarlane *29, 32*
MacGilps *220*
Bertie MacGregor *30, 31*
Tearlach MacGregor *177*
Donald Alec MacKechan *275*
Archie Mackechnie *233*
Duncan MacKeith *196*

MacKeiths *237*
Agnes MacKenzie *176*
Murdo Mackenzie *68*
John MacKinnon *326*
Alasdair MacLean *230, 282*
Donald MacLean *178, 187, 207*
Eliza and Margaret MacLean *170, 337*
Hughie MacLean *179*
John Maclean *347*
John MacLean *175, 316–19, 361*
Lachie MacLean *190, 209*
Malcolm MacLean *173, 231, 304, 317*
Mary MacLean *171*
Mary & Ellen MacLean *170*
Sorley Maclean *217, 282*
Don'd MacLennan *178*
Rory MacLennan *9, 87*
Lachlan MacLeod *165, 275*
Neil MacPhail *178, 202*
Mary MacVicar *249*
Hamish McCuaig *103, 107, 109*
Donald McDiarmid *121*
Ian McDiarmid *119, 120, 121*
Alan McDougall *47*
Miss McFarlane *33*
Dr. McIntyre *28*
Mr. McKechran *118*
Neil McKinnon *42,*
Donald McLean *190*
John McLean *47–48*
Don'd Meek *173, 178–79, 202*
Peter Morrison *163, 230, 277–82*
Morvern Informants *185*
Mull Informants *183, 188*
John Munro *242, 243*
Mr Pearce *137*
Perthshire Informants *185*
Mrs Ramsay *131*
Jn. Russell *25*
Alasdair Sinclair *177, 210*
Donald Sinclair *50, 171, 172, 177, 178,*
231, 296, 314, 324, 346, 354
Murdoch Sinclair *314*
Skye Informants *217, 218*
Robert Stewart *9, 11, 79*
Sutherland Informants *200, 219*
Tiree Informants *171, 202, 204*
Uist and Benbecula Informants *201*
Mr. Yule *34*
Interviewers
Patrick Boyle *201, 217, 219*
E. R. Cregeen *102, 103*
Donald Archie MacDonald *9, 153, 159,*
165, 233, 234, 240, 263, 265, 267, 278,
John MacInnes *50, 177, 185, 231, 290,*
295, 297, 305
B.R.S.Megaw *103*
Irish Folklore Commission *1, 2*

K

Kelp Industry
Kelping *44, 300*

L

Land raid
Balranald *270-71*

M

Mills
Mill – Horse-driven threshing mill *103*
Mill at Cornaig *329*
Peinmore mill *251*

P

Peats *39, 71, 275, 305, 314*
Photographs *2, 3, 4, 9, 22, 39, 135, 145, 230,*
265, 280, 294, 299, 307, 311, 333, 334
Piping Traditions *318*
Farquharson's Hymns *320*
MacCrimmon *323*
Place-names
Acharacle *231, 288*
Airidh Glas *113*

Ardnamurchan *viii, 90, 147, 227, 231, 255, 287, 289*
Argyll *viii, 55, 92–93, 96, 147, 176, 227, 230, 249, 255, 286, 304, 313, 319, 348–49, 360*
Auchendrain *55, 100, 142, 159, 242, 357*
Auchnagaul *242, 243, 352*
Balaphetrish *294*
Balemartin *62, 175, 178, 199, 203, 210, 299, 307, 318, 323, 347*
Balephetrish *10, 199, 204, 209, 231, 294*
Balevulin *171, 202, 327, 328, 329, 330, 338*
Balivanich *282*
Ballaphetrish *45*
Ballephuil *50*
Balmacara *9, 11, 83*
Balranald *165, 230, 264, 266–74, 281*
Barra *viii, 202, 227, 248, 260, 314–15*
Barrapol *177–78, 198, 203, 212, 332*
Benbecula *viii, 147, 154, 163, 201, 227, 230, 260, 275, 284*
Bridge of Douglas, Kennels *242*
Bruichladdich *118*
Calbost *183*
Calgary *205, 250, 251, 253*
Campbeltown *154, 162, 355*
Caolas *47, 173, 178–79, 202, 205, 207, 212, 308, 310*
Carinish Inn *277*
Carradale *38, 96, 159, 161, 237, 240, 336*
Castlebay *230, 260, 261*
Cnoc Crom *233*
Cornaig *47, 170, 176–77, 206, 213, 231, 302, 306–07, 324, 326, 329–40, 345, 361*
Cornaigbeg *9, 47, 49, 175, 180, 202–03, 206–07, 210, 317, 322, 335, 337, 347, 361*
Cornaigmore *46, 48–49, 177, 179, 199, 203, 210, 343*

Lower Cragabus *101, 103, 105*
Crannich *30, 31*
Crossapol *172–73, 176, 180, 197, 199, 204, 208, 295, 309, 324*
Culloden *239*
Dornie *9, 11, 83*
Eigg *viii, 147, 153, 187*
Glencoe *viii, 227, 287, 297, 314–15*
Glen Gorm Estate *35*
Grimsay *viii, 147, 163, 165, 169, 230, 266, 275, 277–82, 284–85*
Gruline *188, 190, 258*
Hianish *9, 10, 42–44, 173*
Inveraray *55, 142*
Islay *viii, 95, 99–101, 103, 121, 138–39, 143, 225*
Jura *viii, 147, 154, 157, 161, 181, 221, 233–6, 305*
Keills *153–57, 220, 222, 231, 233, 236, 292–93*
Kennovag *62*
Kenoway *33, 307*
Kilmichael *169, 196, 237*
Kilnave *105, 111*
Kintyre *93, 162, 196, 237, 239*
Kirkapoll *61, 63, 65*
Kirkton *11, 83, 86, 87*
Kyles Paible *159, 230, 264, 279, 280*
Lochboisdale *230, 260, 282, 283*
Loch Eport *201*
Loch Glashan *9, 10, 36*
Loch Riaghain *9, 65–66*
Luib *9, 77, 284*
Melness *200, 219*
Minard *57*
Moal nan Ron *115*
Morvern *159, 185, 231, 253, 286, 287, 289, 350*
Muir of Ord *9, 11, 79, 80*
Mull *viii, 7, 9–10, 26–34, 93–95, 105, 115, 147, 156, 164, 168, 183, 186–91,*

227, 245, 249, 253–54, 259, 297, 302, 304–05, 314, 322–23, 330, 345
North Argyll *viii, 227, 230, 286*
North Uist *viii, 147, 159, 163, 201, 227, 249, 263, 277, 284–85*
Oban *161, 177, 188, 197, 210, 243, 283, 286, 320, 337*
Ornaig *38*
Perthshire *viii, 147, 170, 185*
Port Charlotte *119, 131*
Portree *9, 10, 68, 87, 218*
Salen *30–31, 186–90, 253, 297, 303*
Sanaig *100–01, 133, 145*
Sandaig *171, 177, 199, 203, 209, 212*
Sandbank *163, 230, 278, 280*
Scarinish *43, 48, 60, 175, 178–79, 202–03, 212–13, 317, 342*
Scolpaig *265*
Sconser *9, 76*
Skye *viii, 7, 9, 10, 34, 68, 80, 81, 147, 153, 185, 191, 217–18, 221, 249, 269, 322*
Sollas *201, 263*
South Uist *201*
Strathnaver *219*
Sunipol *187, 239*
Sutherland *viii, 147, 194, 200, 219, 320*
Tighgharry *260, 265*
Tiree *viii, 7–10, 33, 42, 46, 49–50, 60, 65, 94, 147, 156, 164, 171–72, 176–77, 180, 192, 197–99, 202–16, 227, 231, 248, 294, 305, 313–21, 327, 330–35, 340, 343–46, 349, 361*
Tobermory *9, 34, 164–65, 187, 189, 190, 245–47, 253–59, 290, 295*
Uigshader *68*
Uisken *168, 188*
West Hynish *171, 297, 299, 307, 314*
Prince Charles *268, 273*

R

Raids, see Land raid

Runrig Tenancy *158–59, 230, 264, 283, 285*

S

School of Scottish Studies Archives
    SA1968/71 – Funeral Ceremonies *256*
    SA 1968/72/73/ 74 – John MacDonald *280*
    SA1968/75 – Peter Morrison *282*
Shieling huts *357*
Sketchs [see also diagrams & illustrations] *10, 66, 106–09, 117, 124, 127, 132, 136, 140*
Social Life *264*
Song, singing
    Song about John MacInnes's father *305*
    Songs *202, 305, 314, 330, 347, 348*
Spinning Wheels *279, 303, 319, 324, 341*
Storytelling, Story
    Cú Chulainn 50
    How the Grey Horse came to Scotland 282
    Story about a former Bailie *328*
    Story of John MacFadyen *321*
    Story of the MacMillans *221*
    Traditional Storyteller, Mull *189*
Supernatural
    Black arts *315*
    Ghost funerals *349*
    Ghostly light *199*
    Second sight *270, 314*
    Sink Ships *315*
Superstitious beliefs
    Beliefs among fishermen *241*
    Evil eye *264, 344*
    Blacksmith magic charms *257*
    Fishermen ritual purification *336*
    Fishermen, superstitions *348*
    Taboo foods *314, 335, 336*
    Unlucky Stone *269*

T

Tacksmen *330*
Traditional Customs
    Coffin-rest *119, 252, 253*
    Cure for jaundice *297*
    Dun Nordridge (February customs) *143*
    Funeral Ceremonies *256*
    Funerals *298, 345, 349*
    Old St Bride's Day *143*
    Weddings customs *335, 345*
Tea *81, 239, 282, 343–55*
Thatched houses *9, 71, 76–77, 260, 268, 310, 342, 369*
    Rush Thatch *68, 369*
Tunes
    Pibroch: 'The Battle of the Pass of Crieff' *48*
    Tune: 'The Raid on Balranald' *230, 270, 318, 323, 361*
Turf Drains *220*

W

Wells
    Prince Charles's *273*
Weather-lore
    Cuckoo storm *245*
    lamb storm *245*
Weavers *320, 321, 341, 342*
Whisky *3, 240, 252, 275, 282, 318, 325, 332*
    Distillery *332*
    Dram *240, 274, 297*
Writers
    Margaret Bennett *3, 5, 6*
    Martin MacGregor *3*
    Seán Ó Súilleabháin *2*
    T. C. Smout *3*

INDEX VOLUME 5
1959-1968

A

Archaeological Sites
    Ring of stones *77*
    Standing Stone at Balenoe *371*

B

Baillidh Mòr, see also Factors *11, 30, 50, 61, 87, 235, 268, 279, 295, 336*
Bards (see Poets)
Broga Fina *240*
Buildings
    Borve castle *423*
    Highest house in Tiree *371*
    Inveraray Castle *214, 290*
    Island House *9, 17, 23, 45, 51, 61, 73, 279*
    Kirkapol Church *364*
    Old Buildings at Cornaigbeg *274*
    Oldest big House in Tiree *61*
    Old houses Benbecula *32, 45, 212, 428*
    Scarinish Church *364*
    The Long House *413*

C

Ceilidh *25, 68, 175, 182–85, 273, 385*
Census
    Census of Balephuil 1851 *48, 58*
    Balephuil families *262*
    Census of Greenhill 1891 *164*
Clanranald Estate *423, 427, 430*
Clearances, see also Evictions *21, 144, 158, 384, 387*
    Calgary *45*
    West Hynish *400*
    Crofters removed to the shore *360*
Cockfights *77*
Cottars *167–68, 179, 205, 428–29*
Crockan *34, 35*
Crofters *3, 18, 30, 50, 92, 101, 106, 115, 152, 168, 179, 195, 198, 203–06, 220, 241, 248, 251, 254, 256, 260, 265–76, 295–96, 336, 354, 357, 360, 365, 374–75, 382, 384, 392, 418, 424–29, 435, 436*
Crofters Act of 1886 *263*
Crofts *9, 19, 23, 44, 48, 75–76, 92, 101, 105, 158, 207, 216, 248, 260–63, 267–68, 275–78, 284–85, 290, 295, 297, 301, 314–317, 320–22, 328, 331–35, 341, 346–47, 350–53, 360, 375, 380–93, 403, 418, 427, 434*
    Moss Reclamation *9*
    Souming *22, 23, 216, 425*
    Township constable *153, 425, 427*
    Sub-tenancy System *277, 423*
Crops, see Food
Cures *16, 175, 190, 193, 235*

D

Diet *18, 19, 31, 45, 267*
Dock strike *293, 329, 337*
Droving
    Falkirk Tryst *253*
Duke of Argyll *137, 160, 169, 214–15, 338, 350, 404, 413*
Dyeing cloth *31*

E

Electricity *13, 21, 72, 85, 86, 275*
Emigration *31, 215, 430*
Eric
    Lily Cregeen *270, 290, 294, 374, 381, 390, 398*
    Nicky Cregeen *390, 398*
    Extra-Mural lectures *9, 60*
    Lecture Programme *57, 102, 234*
Eviction (see also Clearances)
    Lampoon on Patrick Sellers *134*

F

Factors (see also Baillidh Mòr)
    Bailidh Donald *17*
    Factor Geickie, Geikie, Kiki *56, 65, 87*
    Lampoon on Patrick Sellers *134*

Famine
    Potatoes failed *268*
    Potato famine *18, 20, 87, 214, 418, 430*

Farms, Farming
    Baugh Farm *300*
    Castleton Farm *251*
    Cattle *3, 29, 46, 53, 67, 76, 79, 95, 103, 115, 216, 218, 248, 251, 253, 256, 268, 356, 392, 402, 413, 425, 426*
    Cattle Sale at Crossapol *357*
    Common Grazing *103, 115, 172, 203, 216, 248, 250–51, 278, 332*
    Corn *29, 41, 102, 167–68, 178, 188, 196–97, 208–09, 218, 297, 342, 384*
    Cowal farmers *254*
    Cragabus Farm *102*
    Farm servants *240*
    Grasskeepers *425, 426*
    Highland ponies *45*
    Keills Farm *74*
    Kelp *31, 55, 73, 88, 148, 175, 328*
    Lazy-beds *39, 40–41, 275, 415, 420–21, 427*
    Mid Danna Farm *117*
    Peats *81, 245, 278*
    Pigs *30*
    Plough-team *429*
    Scammadale Farm *201*
    Seaweed *39, 40, 73, 105, 415, 420–21*
    Sheep sale *365*
    Subsidies *120*

Farm Implements
    Cas-chrom *39, 41, 93*
    Flail *206, 417*
    Quern *40, 41, 250, 267, 427*
    Scythe *196, 342*
    Spade *39, 41, 92, 114, 116, 196, 421*
    Thrashing Mill *417*

Ferry *120, 254*

Fishermen, Sailors & Boats
    Boat-builder *280*
    Boats *21, 29, 75, 78, 204, 217, 249, 359*
    Skiffs *249*
    Fishermen *29, 32, 148, 155, 204, 248, 331–34, 389, 402–03*
    Fishing *21, 31–32, 78–79, 141–45, 152, 175, 178–79, 201, 212, 216, 231, 249, 254, 280, 332, 356, 383, 390*
    Fishing disasters *31*
    Ling-fishing *32, 332*
    Manx fishing boat *79*

Food (see also Diet)
    Barley *45, 418, 426*
    Bread *18, 331*
    Butter *18, 149, 267, 426*
    Cod *19, 249, 332*
    Cooking and Preserving *255*
    Fish *18–19, 132, 145, 179, 200, 235, 249, 253, 267, 281*
    Oats 18, *195–96, 206, 250, 426*
    Porridge *18, 240, 267*
    Potatoes *18, 39, 75, 84, 196, 203, 206, 216, 222, 250, 253, 267–68, 286, 363, 426, 428*
    Rye *426*

G

Gaelic *19, 22, 25, 43, 54-55, 58, 68, 89–90, 93–94, 97–99, 106, 109, 128, 133, 138–39, 147, 150, 152, 155–56, 165, 187, 204, 207, 215, 225–26, 231, 243, 252, 269–70, 327, 35–53, 361, 388, 409, 425, 441, 450*

Gaelic Poem to the Earl of Argyll *215*

Genealogy
    John Brown descent of the Cooper *355*
    Mrs. Black Family History *359*
    Hector Kennedy Family *367*

Sinclair genealogy *153*
Glasgow Corporation *64*

I

Informants
    Miss Caroline Black *374, 378*
    Charles Brown *261, 263, 265, 273, 296, 355, 432*
    John Brown *263, 285, 290, 295, 301, 340, 343, 350–55, 375, 378, 381, 386, 393–95, 399–400, 432, 438*
    Duncan Campbell *198, 203, 215–21, 247*
    John Campbell *23, 30, 235, 240, 300*
    Maggie Campbell *231, 247, 410*
    Mary Anne Campbell *20, 23, 25*
    Miss Kit Campbell *200*
    Sandy Campbell *74, 78, 97, 200, 333, 335, 439*
    Mary Fraser *207, 287*
    Duncan Graham *115, 195, 198, 204, 222, 231*
    Daisy and Jessie Gray *140*
    Angus Henderson *130, 141*
    Donald Kennedy *369, 370*
    Hector Kennedy *43, 49, 52, 54, 62, 68–69, 70–73, 146, 150, 158, 163, 173–74, 177, 182, 189, 261–63, 269, 272–75, 285–86, 290, 299, 334, 337, 343, 363–67, 378, 380, 391, 398, 439*
    Dugald MacArthur *333, 339–40, 439*
    Malcolm MacAskill *41*
    Eddie MacCallum *207, 290, 410*
    Calum MacDonald *11, 49, 60, 65, 87, 176, 191, 261, 341, 350, 384*
    Donald Eoghan MacDonald *291, 416*
    John MacDonald *41, 84, 119, 213, 294ff.*
    Malcolm MacDonald *27, 434–36*
    Donald Alex MacEachan *291, 416, 422*
    Mrs MacInnes *94–97*
    Donald Mackeachnie *237*
    Archie MacKechnie *81, 110, 117, 211, 244, 290, 408*
    Donald Mackechnie *135, 237, 272*
    Duncan MacKeith *232*
    Agnes Mackenzie *9, 364*
    Donald Mackenzie *127, 133, 224, 270, 274, 298, 327, 389*
    Mrs Mackenzie *34, 37, 49, 54, 65, 87, 142, 161–62, 175–76, 180, 259*
    Ronnie MacLauchlan *95, 108, 194, 201–02*
    Alex MacLean *138, 236*
    Calum Maclean *66, 440*
    Donald MacLean *38, 44*
    Eliza MacLean *31*
    John Maclean *22, 30, 36, 49, 55–56, 62, 190, 218, 273, 397*
    Margaret MacLean *21*
    Mary and Ellen MacLean *165, 363*
    Mrs. MacLean *388*
    MacLean Sisters *21, 46, 363*
    Alisdair MacLeod *100*
    Lachlan MacLeod *39, 41, 291, 415, 420*
    Doctor Angus MacNiven *234, 239*
    Alick Hector Macphail *59*
    Archie MacVicar *90, 224–25, 257, 405*
    Hamish McCuaig *102*
    Donald Meek *187–89*
    Donald Morrison *128, 132*
    Peter Morrison *40–41*
    Donald Sinclair *13, 24, 27, 31, 33, 35–37, 43–44, 48, 51–52, 56, 58, 61, 66, 68, 70, 73, 118, 146, 148, 151–52, 154, 157, 160, 163, 169–70, 175, 178–79, 181–83, 187, 190, 193, 259, 262, 270–75, 283, 297, 301, 327, 329, 354, 369–70, 375, 379, 393–94, 435, 440*
    Arthur Sutherland *219, 227, 230*
    Tearlach White *143–46, 177–81, 290, 342, 398, 406*
Interviewers

Donald Archie MacDonald 89, *423*
Rev. Donald Mackenzie *127, 133, 224, 270, 274, 298, 327, 389*
Morag Macleod *234*

K

Kelp industry
    Kelp-making *31, 148*

L

Land Court *101, 169, 217–19, 403*
Land League *50, 150, 158, 167, 173, 175, 403*
Land League agitation *158, 403*
Land League riots *150*

M

Rev. Donald MacCallum monument *171–72*
Manx Graves *120*
Mills *22–23, 253, 427*
Mining
    Nickel Mine *411*

N

Nickname *144*

P

Paintings of Tiree
    Duncan Macgregor White *177–78, 342*
Photographs *26, 51, 57, 73, 102, 117, 129, 132, 144, 157, 181, 194, 197, 222–23, 239, 286, 290, 297, 341, 391, 407–08*
Piping Traditions
    Duncan Lamont *93, 128, 234*
Place-names
    Airdveg *291, 422*
    Ardnamurchan *171*
    Ardnastruban *39, 41, 415*
    Ardrishaig *219, 227, 229, 249*
    Argyll *89, 123, 136, 169, 172, 176, 194–95, 214–15, 231, 243, 350, 406, 408*
    Auchindrain *410–13*
    Auchterarder *89, 127, 270, 298*
    Aulds *416*
    Barr a bhalla *207*
    Balemartin *157–58, 181, 186, 190–92, 268, 273, 283, 294, 301, 316–17, 320–23, 333–34, 339–41, 350–51, 370, 385, 396, 434–36, 439*
    Balemartine *11, 17, 27, 49, 62, 73, 291, 440, 441*
    Balenvoe *334*
    Balephetrish *25, 28, 30, 49, 52, 57, 88, 90, 146, 151, 299, 300, 370*
    Balephuil *27, 34–37, 44, 48, 51–54, 58, 60, 72–73, 143, 153, 157, 164, 170–71, 177, 179–80, 259–66, 270, 273, 275, 284–86, 290, 296–98, 301–05, 308–11, 329, 334–35, 339, 342–43, 351–52, 358ff.*
    Balevullen *350, 379, 387, 394, 438*
    Balevullin *20, 25–26*
    Balranald *416–18*
    Barra *97, 153, 294, 332, 430*
    Barrapol *25, 38, 43–44, 46, 55, 71, 73, 159, 165, 168, 243, 371, 392, 403*
    Benbecula *39, 291, 415–16, 422–27, 430*
    Bradleys Cave *132*
    Burnside *216, 219–21, 230–31, 361*
    Caolas *11, 49, 60–61, 187*
    Carabus *106*
    Cornaigbeg *22–23, 30, 32, 55, 143, 193, 274–78*
    Cornaigmore *23, 32, 59, 274*
    Crarae *91, 224–25*
    Creagorry *39*
    Crossapol *9, 23, 34, 49, 65, 72, 161, 167, 175, 259, 274, 277, 331, 351–52, 356, 364, 390*
    Dervaig *93, 135, 136–37, 237*
    Grimsay *5, 39–41, 93, 290–91, 415, 420, 421*
    Gruline *127, 138, 236*

Heylipol *43, 49*
Hilipol *52, 62, 69, 158, 160, 169, 277, 299, 339*
Hillview *293*
Hynish *13, 27–29, 45, 48, 52, 54, 59, 157, 182, 185–86, 259, 262, 270–72, 277, 284, 290, 294, 296–98, 326–27, 332–33, 336, 344–45, 353–54, 356, 370, 375, 378, 383, 388, 391–95, 398–403, 439*
Hynish and Mannal *356*
Inveraray *61, 154, 214–15, 290, 404, 412, 414–15*
Inverary *56, 89, 214*
Islay *30, 76, 102, 106–07, 129, 132, 211, 224, 243, 294, 299*
Jura *74, 76, 81–87, 98–99, 117–20, 212, 218, 245, 281, 294*
Keills *74–79, 81, 84–85, 94–98, 108–09, 113, 117, 120, 194–95, 200, 211, 244, 290, 407, 408*
Kilkenneth *167, 171–72, 331, 359*
Kilmoluag *185, 371*
Kilmoluaig *38, 44–45, 88*
Kirkapol *30, 189, 262, 282, 300, 338*
Kirkpol *364*
Kyles Paible *41*
Linne Mhuirich *108*
Lochgair *89, 90, 92–93, 204, 224–25, 257, 405*
Lochgilphead *89, 101, 113, 195, 215, 217, 247, 252, 256–57, 409*
Loch Sween *74, 97, 108*
Mallaig *249*
Manitoba *164, 190, 335, 430*
Mannal *28, 60, 157, 191, 270, 272, 290, 293–95, 314–15, 331–32, 335–39, 356–61, 370, 381–88, 401, 403, 407, 438, 439*
Mull *26–29, 33, 55–56, 61, 88, 90, 123, 127, 129, 134, 136, 138, 190, 214–15, 234, 237–40, 257, 268, 280–81, 294, 360*
Newfoundland *140*
North Uist *40, 209*
Oban *24, 66, 69, 131, 154, 194, 199, 239, 290, 365–66, 406, 415*
Perthshire *19*
Sandaig *36, 46, 72, 154, 165, 191, 265, 331, 356, 367*
Scarinish *9, 88, 274, 282, 364*
Shetland *227–28, 230, 253*
Shirvan estate *205*
Shirvan Estate *115*
Silvercraigs *101, 113, 114, 116, 118, 195, 196, 199, 203–07, 215–23, 227, 229–31, 247, 248–55, 287*
Silvercraigs Sketch map *219, 221*
Skye *5, 26, 55, 100, 119, 136, 172, 187, 243, 294*
Sleive *301, 339, 351, 380–81, 385, 391, 393*
Sliabh *267*
Sollas *40*
Soroby *17, 27–28, 35, 57, 73, 189, 282*
Soroby graveyard *27*
South Uist *300, 421–23*
Sunipol *30, 56, 137, 233*
Tigh-Voulen *108*
Tiree *7, 9, 11, 23, 28–30, 34–35, 43, 47–48, 55, 56–65, 69–70, 73, 87–90, 118, 123, 127, 136, 142–43, 145, 151, 157, 162, 166, 172, 176–85, 192–94, 214–15, 226, 235–36, 243, 257, 259, 280–84, 289–93, 299–32, 342, 351–52, 356–57, 360–61, 372, 399, 404, 406–07*
Tobermory *130, 138, 140–43, 191, 293, 337*
Traigh Solbhaig *327*

Uisken *128, 132*
Uist *30, 40, 103, 209, 289–90, 294, 300, 415, 421–23*
Ulva *74, 79, 80, 95, 130–32*
West Hynish *13, 48, 52, 182, 259, 284, 290, 297, 326–27, 344–45, 353–54, 375, 378, 392–93, 399–400*
Poets (see also Bards)
    Colin MacDonald *262, 273, 379, 388, 396, 399*
    Mary Macdonald *164*
    Mary MacDougal *189*
    John MacLean *21, 158–59, 163, 181, 184–85, 189, 190, 192, 199, 268, 273, 275–76, 334–35, 380, 385*

R

Religion
    Free Kirk *95, 139, 140, 252*
Research at Inveraray *215*
Runrig *97, 101, 114, 195–96, 203,* 205, *212, 216, 279, 286, 424, 429*

S

School of Scottish Studies Archives
    SA 1970/361 & 362 – Archie McKechnie *94*
    SA1970/363-8 – Wilma Dixon and Alasdair MacLeod *99*
    SA1971/79-99 – Mull and Tiree *127*
    SA 1971/ 198 – Ronnie MacLauchlan *202*
    SA 1971 /201 – Archie MacKechnie *211*
    SA1971/202 – Runrig at Silvercraigs *203*
    SA1971/286 – Archie MacVicar *225*
    SA1972/78/79 – Donald Sinclair *259*
Sheiling *413, 425*
Social links *118*
Songs, Singing
    Songs *22, 24–26, 43, 58–59, 62, 68, 70, 91, 94, 98, 100, 129, 138, 144, 159, 163–64, 166, 181, 183, 185–86, 189–90, 193, 236, 241–42, 262, 271–73, 283, 285, 335, 340, 343, 352, 417, 418–19*
Spinning *31, 95, 96, 231, 242*
Storytelling, Story
    Anecdote – John MacDonald *336*
    Anecdotes *49, 67*
    Barrhormid light *111*
    Boundary dispute *47*
    Clann na h-Oidhche 133, 136
    Ghost Story of Balranald *15, 417*
    Shetland Story *227*
    Stories *17, 24–25, 27, 33, 35, 49, 58–59, 68, 87, 99–100, 108–09, 136, 139, 156, 164, 171, 176–77, 187, 273, 299, 371, 418, 428*
    Stories of Finn and Oscar and Cuchuillin *428*
    Stories of the Fairies *156*
    Story about *Niall na h-oidhche 236*
    Story Battle of the Sheaves *21*
    Story of Campbell of Knock *237*
    Story of Clearance in Glen Aros *238*
    Story of John MacInnes's father *47*
    Story of the Baillidh Mòr *9, 54*
    Story of the factor Maclaurine *65*
    Story of the killing of a Torloish heir *136*
    Story of the Maclauchlans *237*
    Story of the White Horse *225*
Supernatural
    Banhormid light *111*
    Fairies *25, 28, 156, 175, 225, 256*
    Ghost funerals *15*
    Ghostly light *97*
    Ghosts *20, 33, 175*
    Greenhill house haunted *53*
    Lights at Brenchoille *414*

Monsters at Greenhill *67*
Mysterious light *109, 110*
Poltergeist *150*
Predictions: John MacLean *21*
Second sight *15, 16, 52, 65,* 136, *160, 161, 176, 183, 369*
Witchcraft *49, 76, 84, 87, 109, 120, 136, 149, 171, 241–42, 256, 413*

Superstitious beliefs
    Charms *149, 162, 193*
    Evil eye *52, 179, 201*
    Fishing taboos *141*
    The Stone at Ruaig *11*
    The Witch's House *413*

T

Tacksmen 30, 88, 423-29,
Tackety boots *240*
Tea *21, 35, 49, 53, 78, 149, 173, 192, 204, 247, 257, 283, 335, 342*
Thatched houses *21, 36, 74, 102, 113, 143–44, 165, 181, 248, 338, 340, 342, 371, 408, 428*
Tinkers in Tiree *176*
Tiree documentation *404*
Township constable *153, 425, 427*
Traditional Customs
    Cailleach – Last sheaf *29, 188, 210, 252*
    Clan Traditions *423*
    Funeral Customs *59, 164, 235*
    Harvest Customs *209*
    Harvest Maiden *188, 192, 287*
    Keening *160, 164*
    Marriage *9, 21, 24, 277, 339*
    Marriage negotiations *21, 24*
    New Year *19, 45, 175, 192, 216, 232, 242, 257, 370*
    New Year and Christmas customs *175*
    Sabbath *372*
    St. Bridget's Day *192*
    Traditions *22, 36, 43, 100, 108–09, 157, 161, 166, 234, 238, 423*
    Wakes *53, 238*
    Wedding Celebrations *21, 55–56, 70, 105, 144–45, 148, 174*

W

War
    World War I *366–67, 438*
    World War II *369*
Waulking Cloth *166*
Weaving *31, 95, 133, 231*
Wells
    Mary's Well *15*
    St. Patricks Well *13*
    Well at Achantiobairt *413*
Whisky *3, 22, 25, 37, 43, 53, 68, 88, 119, 149, 154, 156, 183, 185, 208–11, 233, 235, 238, 242, 353*
    Distillery Tobermory *141*
    Distilling *154, 287*
    Dram *50, 352*

INDEX VOLUME 6
1973-1974

A

Agrarian & Social Life in Benbecula *25*
Animals
    Clydesdale horses *137, 157*
    Highland cattle *77, 137, 139*
    War horses *137*

B

Baillidh Mòr *45, 170, 200, 227, 237, 293*
Bards (see also Poets) *69–70, 74, 83, 100, 104, 107–10, 125, 136, 175, 182, 205, 207, 209, 223–24, 265, 273, 289, 304–05, 310*
Board of Agriculture *89*
Botanical notes of Sir George *40*
Bridges *219–20*
Buildings
    Balephuil oldest building *50*
    Black house *269*
    Cooper's house *188*
    Eilean Donan *116*
    Gott Manse *65, 152*
    Rev. Duncan Macdougall house *51*
Burial sites
    Burial Ground at Kirkapol *287*
    Burial Ground at Soroby *288*
    Burial Stones at Balephuil *289*
    Graveyard *70, 216, 232, 265, 283–84*

C

Cachaile, cachalla (gate) *60–62, 65, 73–75, 79–91, 96–97, 102, 129, 150, 275*
Cairn *219, 221*
Clearances [see Eviction]
    Kilmoluag *90*
    MacColl expelled Catholics from Tiree to Barra *205*
    Mannal *148*

Campbells at Crarae *39*
Cooperative schemes *87*
Cottars 20, *42, 46,* 62, 77, 89, *97,* 110, *179–80, 321–22*
Crofters 15, *20–21, 26–30,* 42, 53, 62, *77–78,* 87, 89, 92, 99, *110, 140, 161, 169, 179, 230, 246, 248–49, 268, 273, 275, 293, 299, 310*
Crofts *19, 21, 30,* 62, 73, 89, *102–03, 107, 142, 147–50, 169, 185, 244, 247, 262, 271, 273, 292, 296, 299, 302, 307, 312*
Crops (see Food)
Cures *145, 150, 215, 238*

D

Diet *238, 279*
    Porridge & cream *251*
Droving
    Falkirk Tryst *66, 183*
Duke of Argyll
    Deeds of Tiree *139*
    Duchess, Matilda *33*
    Duke *viii, 7, 23, 32–33, 35, 39, 41–43, 46, 51, 114, 266, 287, 294, 297*
    Funeral of the Duke of Argyll *23, 32*
    Headstone *35*
    Permission for access to the archive *39*

E

Eric's Lectures 36
Eric's family
    Lily Cregeen *13, 18, 87*
    Kirsty *87, 245, 251, 255*
    Charles Radcliffe *257*
Eviction, *see* Clearances
    Emigrant ship *120, 148, 207*
    MacColl expelled Catholics from Tiree to Barra *205*

F

Factor (see Baillidh Mòr
Famine

Potato Famine *221, 284*
Potato failure of 1860 *190*
Farms, Farming
    Cattle sales *92*
    Common Grazing *26, 54, 73, 77*, 102, *185, 247, 285*
    Ear-marks in lambs *28*
    Fidden Farm *238*
    Grasskeeper *21, 26*
    Grazing committee *53, 68, 77*
    Herding *20–21, 26, 55–56, 61, 73, 75–76, 84–85, 128–29, 139, 200, 272*
    Herd-boys *273*
    Horse-dealers *92*
    Hough Farm *140*
    Kelp *28, 71, 79, 141, 149–50, 195, 261, 263, 279, 295*
    Knock farm *236*
    Lazy-beds *9, 10, 15, 18, 52, 83, 130*
    Machair *15, 25, 30, 54, 97, 200, 286, 296*
    Milking *15, 55, 61, 63, 72, 76, 85–86, 176, 196, 202–03, 248, 273*
    Seaweed *10, 28, 52–53, 71, 130, 140, 150, 161, 176, 180, 221, 292*
    Soumings *54, 56, 102*
    Township bull *16, 19, 26, 56*
    Town-herd at Bailephuil *55*
    Township shepherd *20*
    Trade in pigs and dairy products *29*
Farm Implements
    Cas-chrom *10–17, 52, 232*
    Cromags *69*
    Flails *47, 69*
    Reaper-binder *143*
    Scythe *248*
Filming projects *14, 17*
    Filming John Brown *309*
Fishermen, Sailors & Boats
    Cod *251*
    Ferry-boats *167*
    Fishing *67, 74, 171, 243–44, 261, 296*
    Kippers *244*
    Marie Stuart schooner *64, 165*
    Smacks in Scarinish harbour *165*
    Shipyards *252*
    Steamers *166–67, 300*
Food (see also Diet))
    Barley *15*
    Cheese *23, 247*
    Meat *252*
    Oats *15*
    Porridge *251*
    Potatoes *15, 18, 22, 52, 71, 76, 84, 89, 97, 130, 143, 179, 221, 246, 285*
    Scones *251, 303*

G

Gaelic *11, 17, 38, 57, 59–60, 67, 71, 74, 76, 82, 86, 92, 98, 101, 110, 116–19, 121, 126–27, 135, 145, 147, 151, 153–54, 164, 174, 187, 218, 223–24, 249–50, 254, 275, 294, 297, 301, 307–08, 311, 315, 324, 328*
Genealogy
    Cooper Family *47, 49–50, 56, 98, 100, 105, 107, 118, 121, 124, 138, 145, 188, 196, 278, 303*
    Genealogy of families in Benbecula *29*
    Ian Mac Ailein family *283*
    John MacLean Forbears *281*
    MacEachern Family Origins *181, 193, 194*
    MacPhail family & croft *297*

I

Informants
    John Brown *48–49, 67–69, 78, 82, 98, 100–01, 104, 107, 110, 120, 128, 141, 163, 169, 174, 189, 195, 259, 262, 276–77, 292, 297, 305–09*
    Margaret Brownlee [Brownlie] *211, 215*
    Neil Brownlee [Niall Brownlie] *199, 201, 215, 216, 217*

Maggie Campbell *115, 243*
Duncan Colville *218–19*
Angus Henderson *160, 230, 237, 241*
Donald Alasdair Johnson *10–14, 18, 130*
Hector Kennedy *45, 68–69, 78, 89, 104, 107, 120, 128, 136, 175, 185, 192, 197, 260, 266, 278, 292, 309*
Mary Kennedy *58, 76, 78, 144, 306*
Attie MacCallum *236–37*
Archie Macdonald *9, 31, 65, 69, 274*
Calum MacDonald *80, 97, 104, 151, 189, 205, 213, 230, 261, 270*
Donald Eoghan MacDonald *12*
Donald Ewan MacDonald *24, 29, 130*
John Macdonald *12, 18, 22, 130, 183, 210, 293, 294*
Donald Alex MacEachan *17, 22, 25, 130*
Hugh MacEachern *153, 174, 180–82, 216*
Archie MacKechnie *113, 210*
Mrs Mackenzie *64, 94–95, 142, 146*
Donald MacLean *139, 179, 202*
John MacLean *59, 60, 64, 70, 78, 88, 93, 95, 102, 104, 107, 109, 124, 128, 136, 138, 144, 147, 157, 161, 163–64, 175, 177, 179, 186, 192–93, 202, 267–68, 277, 280–82, 287–88, 294, 300, 305, 312–13*
Margaret MacLean *70, 155, 181, 283*
Miss Anne Maclean *118–19, 190*
Lachlan MacLeod *9, 12, 18, 130*
Doctor Angus MacNiven *238, 241*
Duncan MacPhail *98, 105, 142–43, 187–90, 302, 308*
Mrs Mairi MacPhail *161*
Naomi Mitchison *220*
Donald Morrison *227, 231*
Donald Sinclair *49–50, 58–59, 73–74, 78–80, 88–90, 104, 108–09, 120–24, 144, 163, 189, 196, 206, 259–62, 267, 277, 294, 301, 304, 310*

Father Webb in Barra *218*
Tearlach Whyte *112, 208–09, 260*
Interviewers
John MacInnes *23*
Donald Archie MacDonald *9, 12, 31, 130*
Maggie Mackay *44, 135, 187, 199, 208, 215*
Donald Mackenzie *32, 44, 57–59, 74, 82, 223, 227, 229, 242*
Invereray Castle Archives *114*
Tiree papers *114, 209, 210*
Irish Folklore Commission *1, 2, 256*

K

Kelp Industry
Kelp-manufacture *28, 79, 279*
King of Moss *268*

L

Lady Victoria Campbell *239*
Land Court *53, 321*
Land-League *46, 62, 91, 201, 310, 321–22*
Land raid *30, 321, 327*
Balephetrish *78, 89, 107, 286*

M

Manx *254–56*
Manx Gaelic Service *254*
Medical Survey of Tiree population. *191*
Mills *201, 216, 251, 265, 292*
Mòd *224*
Mortality (children) *265*

P

Peat *175, 200, 230*
Photographs *18, 24, 88, 112, 124–25, 129, 155, 161, 186, 195–96, 209, 301*
Piping Traditions
Dond Mackinnon *184*
Neil Maclean *181, 183*
Pipe Major Hector Maclean *183*
Pipe & Fiddle Music *184*

Pipe tune – D.E. MacDonald *24*
Ronnie McCallum – Duke's Piper *33*
'The Campbells are Coming' – Pibroch
   Ronnie McCallum *33*
Place-names
  Aird *17, 27, 115, 130, 181*
  Airdveg *25*
  America *49, 59, 137*
  Ardmhor *14, 18*
  Ardnamurchan *190*
  Ardnastruban *9, 130*
  Ardrishaig *41, 115, 209, 244*
  Argyll *7, 23, 32, 36–37, 133, 139, 154,*
    181, 193, 208, 241, 243, 250, 258
  Auchindrain *36, 39*
  Australia *161, 182, 235, 295*
  Balemartin *55, 60, 62, 70, 74, 83, 91,*
    104, 107, 110, 123, 136, 147–48, 171,
    183, 189, 194, 215, 267, 270–73, 279,
    282, 293–94, 297–98, 310
  Balenoe *75, 97, 104, 136, 291, 295*
  Balephetrish *61, 63, 75, 88–89, 102, 107,*
    135, 154, 159, 161, 177, 181–82, 194,
    196–98, 235, 258, 281, 286
  Balephuil *47–50, 54–55, 60, 62, 74–76,*
    80–83, 101, 104–07, 112–13, 118,
    120–21, 129, 136, 138, 142, 145, 163,
    174–75, 182, 186–88, 193, 198, 200,
    204, 209, 260, 263, 266, 283ff.
  Balevullin *46, 61, 67, 104, 137, 150, 171,*
    185, 187, 194, 268, 285, 296, 311, 313,
    315
  Balinoe *55*
  Balnacraig *79, 109*
  Balranald *12, 24, 29–30, 130*
  Barra *74, 79, 109, 171–72, 195, 205,*
    212, 218, 239
  Barrapol *69, 90, 104, 128, 138–39, 196,*
    199–206, 274, 279, 282–83, 293–94,
    309ff.
  Benbecula *16–17, 25, 28–29, 77, 98, 130*
  Ben Hynish *83, 294*
  Brandon (Canada) *95*
  Calgary (Canada) *50, 188, 235, 303*
  Canada *44, 95, 100, 112, 120, 136, 137,*
    148, 214, 271, 303
  Caolas *67–68, 88, 97, 103, 135, 146–49,*
    197, 213, 305
  Castleton *115, 243, 248–49*
  Clunary *39*
  Cornaigbeg *59–61, 65, 67, 86–88, 93,*
    102, 104, 128, 153, 159–63, 174, 177,
    231, 280–82, 288, 291, 312–13
  Craignish *135, 264*
  Crossapol *61, 94, 106, 142, 264, 281,*
    283, 293
  Dervaig *155, 230, 283, 313*
  Druimfuar *246*
  East Hynish *58, 98, 143*
  Edinburgh *22–23, 33, 47, 100, 189, 232*
  Furnace *36–37, 39*
  Glasgow *12, 29, 37, 44, 96, 100, 126,*
    137, 146–50, 156, 159, 167, 191–92,
    199, 212–13, 223–25, 258, 262, 277,
    290, 297
  Greenhill *58, 67, 75, 79, 92, 128, 217,*
    284, 287, 295, 310–13
  Grimsay *9, 14, 18–19, 130*
  Hianish *101, 142*
  Hilipol *97, 136, 178, 315*
  Hosta *30*
  Hynish *48, 54, 58, 73, 80, 83, 86, 98, 104,*
    143–44, 170, 183, 191–92, 262, 291,
    294, 307, 309
  Inverness *27, 105, 118–21, 190*
  Islay *40, 190, 261, 272*
  Isle of Man *133, 168, 254*
  Keills *42, 113–14, 252*
  Kenovay *93, 100, 139, 161, 189, 197,*
    265, 281, 284, 315
  Kenvara *80, 195, 200, 204, 215, 281*
  Kilmoluag *45, 61, 69, 76, 90, 104, 128,*

138, 144, 159, 163, 185–86, 197, 201, 211, 268ff.
Kinlochleven *160*
Kintyre *219*
Kirkapol *65, 70, 72, 96, 103, 152, 154–55, 165, 167, 171, 173, 186, 194, 265, 282–84, 287*
Larbert *199, 211*
Loch Fyne *244*
Lochgilphead *36, 39, 44, 116–17, 244, 248, 252, 258*
Lòn a bhaisde *303*
Luing *96, 147*
Manitoba *109, 136–37, 170, 175, 184, 267, 271, 294*
Mannal *62, 91, 128, 148, 185, 199, 290, 292*
Mull *42, 44, 68–69, 109, 113, 123, 133, 135, 155, 175, 183, 227, 234–40, 258, 291, 296–97, 316, 317*
New Zealand *155–56, 161, 183–84, 284*
North Uist *22, 115, 130*
Orillia, Ontario *216*
Orkney *91*
Ottawa *216*
Otter Ferry *116*
Paible *12, 18, 21, 130*
Peel *133, 254–57*
Pictou – Nova Scotia *208*
Port Ulbha *264*
Quyeish *97*
Saddell *220*
Salem *227, 229, 238, 241*
Sandaig *75, 79, 104, 128, 141, 179, 184, 200, 202, 212, 217*
Scarinish *45, 47, 60–65, 69, 75, 88, 94–95, 103, 123, 139, 142–44, 163, 165, 168–73, 224, 290, 300, 301, 316*
Silvercraigs *117, 243, 245, 248–50, 251*
Soroby *265, 271, 287–90*
South Uist *10, 14, 77, 130*

St. Kilda *138, 167, 190*
Tigharry [Tigheary] *29–30*
Tiree *viii, 7ff.*
Tobermory *47, 79, 113, 160, 167, 229–32, 238, 241*
Toronto *137, 217*
Uist *viii, 7–10, 14, 19, 22, 24, 28, 77, 115, 130, 167, 232*
Ulva *229, 232, 236, 239, 264, 293*
Vancouver *215–16*
West Hynish *58, 73, 80, 144*
Plant-lore
    Root used for tanning leather *306*
Poets (see also Bards)
    Hector Cameron *217, 223–25*
    Neil MacLaine *125, 224*
    Maclean bardic family *138*

R

Raids, see Land raids
Religion
    Baptists *303*
    Free Church *190, 234, 249, 250, 310*
Runrig *15, 19, 22, 30, 148, 179*

S

Sayings *205, 211, 239, 242, 307*
School of Scottish Studies Archives *8, 9, 31, 38,* 130, *237*
    Report visit 1973 April *31,* 130
    SA1874/88 – Hector Kennedy *311*
    SA1874/109 – Hector Kennedy *261*
    SA1973/177 & 178 – John MacLean *102*
    SA1974/72, 73, 74 Hector Kennedy *266*
    SA1974/75 – John Brown *277*
    SA1974/76, 77, 78 – Hector Kennedy *278*
    SA1974/79 – Hector Kennedy *292*
    SA1974/80 – Hector Kennedy *293*
    SA1974/81 – Hector *294*
    SA1974/81 – Hector Kennedy *294*

SA 1974/82 – John Maclean *163*
SA1974/82 – John MacLean *300*
SA 1974/83 – John Brown *297, 306*
SA1974/84 – Donald Sinclair *304*
SA1974/85 – Donald Sinclair *305*
SA1974/86 – Hector Kennedy *309*
SA1974/87 – Hector Kennedy *310*
SA 1974/89 – Hector Kennedy *312*

Schools *67, 92, 98, 123, 145, 160, 237–50, 270, 273, 275, 279, 315*

Shebeen *203*

Smith (Blacksmith) *93, 104, 153, 154, 180, 181, 193, 230, 231, 313*
   Smith work in Tiree *157*

Songs, Singing
   'Cagaran O' *224, 225*
   Florrie Caimbeul *295*
   'Manitoba' *294*
   Nan Mackinnon: song to MacColl expelling the R.C. from Tiree to Barra – [Tape 7th June '74] *205*
   'Oran na h-ass' *294, 305*
   'Oran na Van' *268, 278–79, 282, 304, 308*
   Song about Clearances *206*
   'Song to Petrol' [petrol shortage] *295*
   Songs *24, 48, 52, 58, 69–70, 107, 110, 121, 136, 141, 170, 175, 185–86, 196, 205–06, 223–24, 268, 277, 282, 292, 294–95, 301, 304–05, 311–12*
   'The Taeping' *294*
   'Tir nan beann, nan gleann 's nan breacan' *294*

Storytelling, Story
   Stories *11, 13–14, 49–50, 56, 71, 80, 110, 124, 126, 130, 159,* 186, *200–01, 212, 235, 237, 256, 279, 310, 317*
   Story of a man going for whisky *204*
   Story of Bacach na Crochaidh *201*
   Story of barefooted woman *202*
   Story of evicting a blind man *201*
   Story of tailor & the witch *202*

Story of the cats *14*
Story of the cave at Kenvara *204*
Story of two cailleachs *203*
Storyteller: Domhnall MacLachlainn Mhòir *71*
Story about Loch a' phuill *205*
Supernatural story *80*
The story of the Barra witch *212*

Supernatural
   Fairy knoll *204*
   Fairy women *200*
   Ghost *49, 63, 80, 124, 278*
   Haunting at Greenhill *79*
   Manadh *49*
   Second sight *151, 196, 200–02, 213–15, 307*
   Supernatural place *80*
   Warnings before a death *50*

Superstitious beliefs
   Charms *203, 215, 241*
   Witchcraft *200–03, 310*

T

Tacksmen *22, 25, 29, 109, 130, 274, 284, 287, 310*
Tanning leather *306*
Tea *40, 164, 208, 221–22, 240, 256*
Thatched houses *11, 18, 108, 122, 138, 160, 163, 185, 203, 245, 271, 301*
Tinkers in Tiree *69*
Tiree Association *124–25, 223*
Tiree & Mull papers *42*
Traditional Customs
   Corn maiden *174*
   Custom of "cisteadh" *240*
   First Funeral using a car *175*
   Funerals *32, 154, 174–75, 187, 215, 219*
   Hogmanay *171, 220, 323*
   Wakes *196*
   Weddings customs *123*

W

War
- Crimean War *306*
- Peninsular War *235, 294*
- Peninsular War hero *294*
- World War I *30, 64, 78, 107, 137, 172, 250, 306*

Waulking Cloth *80, 130, 145*
- Film of cloth-waulking Uist *16, 130*

Whisky *3, 111, 202–04, 222, 238–39, 279, 310*

Worship *249, 297, 307*

Writers
- Margaret Bennett *3, 5, 6*
- Martin MacGregor *3*
- Seán Ó Súilleabháin *2*
- T. C. Smout *3*

INDEX VOLUME 7
1974-1978

A

Argyll Estate *207*

B

Baillidh Mòr *174, 232, 343*
Bards *190–91, 205, 231, 368, 458*
    Livingstone *190*
    MacCodrum *191*
Blacksmiths *155, 180*
Blanket Washing *347*
Born on a Battlefield *335*
Burial-ground at Kilninian *178*
Old burial ground *208*

C

Cachaile Dubh *179*
Cairns *187*
Calgary Castle *155*
Lady Victoria Campbell *310*
Campbell Massacre of the Lamonts *192*
Campbell traditions *176*
Lady Cathcart *270*
Census *379, 382*
Clearances *viii, 143ff.*
    Achateny *252*
    Ardnamurchan *228, 235*
    Ben Shiant *272, 280, 305*
    Bourblaig *270*
    Calgary *179*
    Camus-na-geall *268*
    Glen Cannal *306*
    Glenconon, Skye *286*
    Ramesaig *289*
    Sguird to Sanna *272*
    Skye *287, 290*
    Ulva *155*
Cottars *156, 448*

Crofters *234, 237, 244, 251–52, 266, 296–97, 327, 363, 398, 439, 443, 448, 451*
Crofts *173, 193ff*
Crofts Succession *444, 451*
    Woman Inherited *451*
Crops (see Food)
Cures *340, 359, 388, 402–06, 434–35*
    Beatons *145, 199–200, 211, 297, 366, 371, 388–90, 403*
    Jaundice *388, 403*
    Medicinal Plants *404*

D

Dewar Manuscript *220*
Diagrams *183, 424–25*
Drawings *425*
Drovers *189–91, 310*
Duke of Argyll *216–23, 310, 343, 352, 394–95*
    8th Duke letters *170, 218, 220, 221*
    Duke Niall Manuscripts *223*
    Dukes and Factors *198*

E

Emigration *204, 337, 365*
    Emigration of Sinclairs from Barrapol *440*
Employment *265*
Evictions, see also clearances
    Captain Fraser, Uig, Skye *286, 289, 297*
    Hugh MacCaskill *156*

F

Factor [see also Baillidh Mòr]
    John MacColl *237, 251–52, 271, 299, 300*
    Patrick Sellar *149, 153, 308*
Farms, Farming
    Achanfraoch Farm *390*
    Baugh Farm *420*
    Bulls, fights *438*
    Burning Tangles *436*
    Common grazing *242, 244, 399, 408*

Corn-kiln *408, 438*
Deer fences *268*
Gallvishill Farm *167*
Grazing *179, 242–44, 257, 287, 373–74, 399, 413*
Kilns *300, 424, 469*
Knock Farm *147, 306*
MacNiven's farm *418*
Miagaig Farm *237*
Seaweed *436*
Souming *251, 439*

Farm Implements
Flail *164, 348, 420*

Fishermen, Sailors & Boats
Haddock *243*
Fishing on a Sunday *160*
Fuadach *325, 381*

Fletchers – ancient rights to the land. *307*
Folklife Surveys *2*

Food
Barley *449*
Diet in Tiree *446*
Fish *160, 446*
Fresh vegetables *447*
Herring and potatoes *175*
Liver *446*
Lobster & crabs *446*
Meat *314, 391, 446*
Milk *163–64, 378, 407, 420, 432–33, 437, 447*
Oats *449*
Porridge *175, 358*
Potatoes *174–75, 287, 358*
Sand eels *446*
Scones *385, 391, 447*
Sharing Food *358*
Whelks and limpets *175, 358, 446*

G

Gaelic *146ff.*
Glen Forsa Estate *307*

Genealogy
Mull and Tiree Families *443*

H

Highland Clearances [see also Clearances] *172, 277, 294*
Houses and Families *412–15*

I

Informants
Donald Beaton *297*
John Brown *324, 349, 354, 357, 361, 365, 379, 402–03, 412, 442–43, 454–55*
Neil Brownlee [Niall Brownlie] *461, 464*
Hugh Cameron *276*
Kate Cameron *269*
Archie Campbell *237, 240, 249, 375*
John Campbell *146–47, 174, 197, 311, 408, 415*
Wilma Dixon *290*
Colin Fletcher *152, 226, 229, 230–33*
Miss Jean Gibson *193*
Angus Henderson *145, 153, 158, 171, 178, 203, 225, 227, 248, 279, 300, 304–05, 315*
Mr Keith *163*
Donald Archie Kennedy *360, 401*
Donald Kennedy *351, 355, 380, 383, 395, 411, 420*
Hector Kennedy *159, 192, 197, 321ff.*
John Kennedy *340, 413*
Atty MacCallum *153, 201, 305*
Donald MacDairmid *267, 271*
Calum MacDonald *154*
Dugald MacDonald *321*
Hector MacDonald *321*
John MacDonald *155, 224, 290, 323, 385, 414, 422–23*
Jonathan MacDonald *295*
Angus MacFarlane *145*
Tearlach and Ina MacGregor *393*

Archie MacKechnie *160, 166, 169, 218, 220–24, 281, 391*
Agnes MacKenzie *446*
Hugh Mackenzie *247, 250, 256, 259, 266, 279*
Mrs Mackenzie *357*
Chrissie MacLean *331, 341, 345–46*
Chrissie and Margaret MacLean *331*
Donald MacLean *314, 333, 335, 340, 368*
Hugh MacLean *172, 178*
John MacLean *210, 221,* 324, *353, 366–69, 376, 385–86,* 408, *449,* 452, *461, 464*
Lachlan MacLean *147, 192, 208*
Alasdair MacLeod *285–86, 290, 296*
Malcolm MacMillan *244, 269*
Angus MacNiven *233, 315*
Captain Hugh MacPhail *247, 272*
Donald MacPhail *181–82, 207*
Duncan MacPhail *369, 458, 460*
Hector and Flora MacPhail *351, 363, 458*
Donald Meek *442*
Donald Morrison *171, 184, 189, 194–95, 203–04, 225, 231, 313*
Maggie Scott *200, 209, 215, 312*
Alasdair Sinclair *426, 445, 461*
Donald Sinclair *323, 362, 382, 405–06, 461*
John Sinclair *360*
Lilian Young *167*
Interviewers
    Anne-Berit Ø. Borchgrevnik *171, 186, 207*
    Patrick Boyle *144, 235, 256, 294, 301, 315*
    Bob Duncan *235, 256–57, 285, 289, 294*
    Margaret A. MacKay *331-349*
    Donald Mackenzie *145, 167, 188, 209, 220, 225, 388, 396, 462, 464*
Islands Historical Society *314*

L

Peter Lamont *339*
Land League *173, 298*
Lecture at Cornaigmore *442*
Lecture at Craignure *304*
Lighthouse at Ardnamurchan *244, 245, 247*

M

Flora MacDonald (farmer) *287, 305*
Martins (Skye) *286, 292*
Mills *175, 180, 274, 333, 450*
Mòd *145, 150, 151, 202*

N

Napier Commission *205*

O

Oslo Institute of Ethnology *171*

P

Packman *447*
Pedlar (see Packman)
Peat *146, 154–55, 163, 195, 205, 295, 392, 407, 449*
Photographs *166, 333, 419–23*
Piping Traditions *429*
    Pipers *176*
    MacCrimmons *176, 289*
Place-names
    Achnaba *256, 285*
    Alberta (Canada) *269, 270*
    Alta Chodle *308*
    Ardnamurchan *143–44, 186, 228, 231, 235, 237–38, 240–46, 250, 266, 294, 299, 329*
    Ardslinguish *280*
    Ardtun *173, 189–90, 193, 195, 197*
    Auchindrain *285*
    Auchterarder *165–67*
    Australia *153, 157, 180, 246*
    Ayrshire *321, 371*

Balemartin *326, 353, 366, 396, 418, 458, 464*
Balephetrish *267, 337, 341, 352, 359, 383, 386–87, 397, 404*
Balephuil *364, 379, 394–96, 407–09, 412, 430, 433, 435, 443, 456*
Balevullin *377, 409, 419, 422, 442*
Barrapol *234, 355, 361, 365, 370–71, 375–99, 407–09, 418, 426, 429, 432–35, 439–40, 445, 456*
Bellanoch *162, 282*
Ben More *208, 310*
Ben Shiant *242, 249, 257, 261, 272, 279, 280, 305*
Bourblaig *250–51, 254, 257, 264, 266, 270, 276, 299*
Bowmore *174, 232*
Bunessan *146, 152, 174, 190, 193, 195, 197, 205*
Burnside *422*
Calgary (Mull) *155, 157–79, 202, 227*
California *440*
Campbeltown *168–69*
Camus-na-geall *268*
Canada *191, 246, 337*
Cluany *285*
Coales *154, 340, 363, 404*
Coire-Mhuchlinn *247*
Coll *146, 156–58, 186, 202, 395, 411*
Cornaig *330–33, 340–42, 351, 356, 438, 450*
Cornaigbeg *267, 334, 338, 367–69, 386, 415, 449, 452*
Crossapol *357, 372, 377, 383, 445–46, 452–53, 461*
Dervaig *155–58, 178, 187, 202, 227, 231*
Druim na Crose *300*
Dun Aros *195*
Dundonald *321, 329*
Duntulm *295, 296*
Edinburgh *145, 176, 191, 197, 240, 349*

Glasgow *187, 196, 213, 272–74, 286, 321, 328–29, 334, 337, 374, 381, 387, 461*
Glen Aros *187, 227, 231*
Glen Bellart *227*
Glen Cainnis *149*
Glen Cannel *144, 148–49, 208, 307, 310*
Glen Cannell *308–11*
Glencoe *213, 236, 277, 313*
Glenconon *286*
Glen Forsa *148–49, 307–08*
Glenorchy *230*
Gometra *145, 226*
Grigadale *244, 246*
Heanish *453*
Hilipol *326, 395–98, 432, 438*
Inveraray *170, 198, 214, 218, 220–23, 254, 285, 294, 394–96*
Iona *147, 152, 198*
Islay *161, 173–75, 202, 218, 232, 325, 366, 369*
Jura *160, 179, 222, 282, 392*
Keills *161, 166–70, 216–21, 224, 281, 289–92*
Kenovay *333, 337, 352, 371–72, 385, 415*
Kenrona *434*
Kenvara *438*
Kenway *452*
Kilbride *290*
Kilchoan *237, 239, 240, 243, 247, 268, 272, 273, 274, 275, 299, 300, 301, 305*
Killiechronan *231*
Kilmartin *187*
Kilmorich *247, 253, 263–64, 267, 279*
Kilmory *250–51, 264*
Kilninian *157–58, 178*
Kintra *210, 215, 230*
Kintyre *166–68, 189, 217, 390*
Knapdale *166, 170*
Kyles Piable *290*
Lioncro *286, 296*

Lochan Ellean *421*
Loch Ba *307, 309*
Loch Buie *148, 150, 307*
Manitoba (Canada) *322–23, 380, 412*
Mannal *370, 385, 422–23, 443, 448, 456*
Mid-Argyll *143–44, 160, 187, 216, 219, 220–21, 281*
Mingary *239–41, 261, 272, 300*
Morvern *153, 235, 250, 280, 299, 306, 314, 355*
Moydart *254*
Mull *7, 143ff.*
Newmilns *331, 345*
New Zealand *252, 321, 329*
North Uist *175, 287, 290, 389*
Ormsaigbeg *240–42*
Ornsaybeg *272–73*
Portolloch *281*
Ross *147, 152, 154, 176–77, 184–85, 191, 197, 204, 211, 231*
Rudha *380, 413*
Salen *145–47, 150, 155, 171, 178, 188, 215, 225, 231, 233, 237, 305, 307, 312*
Salum *453*
Sandaig *384, 418, 439, 442, 457, 465*
Scarinish *351, 355, 370, 376, 380, 383–84, 420, 440, 450, 465*
Sgiaid *239, 279*
Sgiued *247*
Skye *143–44, 148, 154, 173, 194, 197, 224, 263, 286–91, 294–95, 373*
Stirling *145, 213*
Tayvallich *224, 263, 391*
Tiree *7, 154ff.*
Tobermory *145, 154, 159, 178, 180, 186, 201, 225–26, 229, 243, 279, 300, 304, 306, 314, 393, 395*
Torloisk *152, 172, 178, 192, 199, 226, 229, 231*
Torness *181–82, 186, 207*
Torr-ronnaidh *232*

Uig *286-89, 296-97*
Uist *175, 236, 270, 287, 290, 389*
Ulva *146, 154–55, 177–78, 199, 209, 226, 230, 233*
Waternish *297*
West Hynish *360, 400, 412, 417*
Plants
    Wild Iris *180*
Poets, *see* Bards
Poor Relief *198*
Potato famine *147, 175, 204, 288*
Pottery *454*
Poverty *204, 234*
Prince Charlie *253*
Proverb *203*

R

Rheumatism *435*

S

Sayings *153, 204, 222, 281*
School of Scottish Studies Archives
    SA 1966/106 – Funeral traditions *455*
    SA1974/114 & 115 – John Campbell *147*
    SA 1974/116&117 – Salen Mod *151*
    SA1974/118 – Angus Henderson *153*
    SA 1974/ 218 – Chrissie MacLean *350*
    SA1974/ 228 –234 – Balephetrish Bay *387*
    SA/1975 16 &17 – Hector Kennedy *398*
    SA 1975/18 John Brown *402*
    SA 1975/19 – Hector Kennedy *407*
    SA1975/20 – Hector Kennedy *408*
    SA 1975/22 – Hector Kennedy *444*
    SA1975/23 – Hector Kennedy *455*
    SA1976/54&55 – Donald Morrison *184*
    SA/1976/235 – Donald Morrison *189*
    SA 1976 / 236 – Donald Morrison *192*
    SA1976/237 – Donald Morrison *196*
    SA1976/238 – Donald Morrison *198*
    SA 1976/239 – Donald Morrison *204*

SA1976/240 – Maggie Scott *213*
SA1978/46 – Angus Henderson *227*
SA1978/47 – Colin Fletcher *230*
SA1978/48 – Donald Morrison *231*
Sheilings *179–83, 186, 207, 260, 264*
    Airigh na Sliseag *208*
    Sheiling huts at Torness *182*
    Sheiling in Glenmore *181*
    Sheilings in Mull *179*
Smiddy work *180*
SNP *216, 282, 291*
Songs, Singing
    Ann Lorne Gillies *151*
    'Ho-hoirean-hog-is hoiream' *366*
    'Oran an air' a' Bhraxy' by Neil Morrison *190*
    'Oran do'n Bana-heard' by Hector MacDonald *192*
    Song about a tea-clipper *211*
    Song on Tobacco – Mary MacDonald *184*
    Songs *147, 189, 193, 205, 210, 230, 268, 279, 288–89, 330, 343, 360, 428, 458, 464*
    Songs about the clearances *288*
    Songs of Willie MacPhail *464*
    'Tha mi nochd 's a chaolais dhubh' *196*
    'Ushag vey ruy my moalg dhoo' *151*
Storytelling, Story
    Am Piobaire *428*
    Anecdote about the poet MacCodrum *191*
    Anecdotes *210, 250, 464*
    'Battle of the Braes' *298*
    'Cuchulainn' *428*
    Epic of William Livingstone *189*
    Fionn & the heroes *427*
    Satire in 'am Factor Mòr' *184*
    Satire of Doctor MacLauchlan *271*
    Stories *149–53, 175, 177, 180, 185, 191–92, 196–203, 212, 228, 287, 310, 327, 372, 375, 377, 427–30, 448*
    Stories and Songs – Donald Morrison *185*
    Story about a minister Aonghais Dubh Morrison *191*
    Story about the MacPhees *177*
    Story about a baby *428*
    Story of an Irish Princess *149*
    Story of Bidein Goraidh *203*
    Story of the black dog *150*
    Story of the Sith *430*
STV "The Clearances" Documentary *viii, 143, 235, 256, 280, 285, 294–95, 303–04, 306, 314*
Supernatural
    Dreams *210, 212*
    Ghosts tales *191, 195*
    Ghost Story *393*
    Manaidhean *195*
    Old woman & a dog *327*
    Premonitions *434–35*
    Second sight *160*
    Story of the Supernatural *228*
    The Black Dog *153*
    Witchcraft *161*
Superstitious Beliefs
    Evil eye *61, 340, 432, 433*
    Hares *432*
    Healing water *341*
    Mull witch *309*
    Witchcraft *161, 309, 315, 432*
Surnames in Tiree *366*

T

Tacksmen *178, 306,*
Tea *211, 253, 278, 337, 354, 358, 378, 385, 410, 443, 460*
Tenants *234, 240, 307, 372*
Thatched houses *177, 255–56, 262, 295, 407, 413, 417–18, 445*
Tobacco *375*
Traditional Customs

  Funeral Customs in Barra *462*
  Keening in Barra *463*
  Making straw rope *346*
  Old times in Ulva *230*
Tunes
  'The Lorgill Crofters Farewell to Skye'
   289

W

War
  Dunkirk *207*
  Napoleonic Wars *287*
  Skye Brigade at Corunna, *287*
  Waterloo *307, 335, 376, 426, 429*
  World War II
Weaver *382*
Whisky *172, 211, 223, 243, 374–75, 443–44,*
 455–57, 462
Wool *312, 340, 375*
  Crotal (dying) *375*
  Spinning *205, 375*
Writers
  Margaret Bennett *3, 5, 6*
  Martin MacGregor *3*
  Seán Ó Súilleabháin *2*
  T. C. Smout *3*

INDEX VOLUME 8
1975-1976

A

Airneach (Red water disease) *147*
Animals
    Clydesdale *15, 60, 146, 224*
    Highland ponies *15, 60, 146*
    Horses in Tiree *15, 224*
    Horses sales *253*
Argyll estate policy in 19th C. *254*

B

Bàillidh Mòr, see also Factors *131, 138, 305, 328*
Bards *26, 29, 31, 272–73, 276–81, 318, 330, 374*
First bicycle (Tiree) *324*
Buildings
    Blackhouse *226*
    Curious Site at Vaul *12*
    House at Ceannsa *227*
    Foundations of old house [sean bhaile] *105*
    Traditional houses – Balevullen *213*
    Whitewashed house Cornaigbeg *65*

C

Changing surnames to Campbell *219*
First motor car (Tiree) *325*
Census *116, 223, 260, 302, 308*
Clay dolls, children's toys *73*
Clearances (see also Evictions)
    Barra, catholics sent to *60, 108*
    Hilipol *118, 305, 313, 328, 354*
    Mannal *42*
Club-land *36, 104, 283, 366*
Cottars *22, 35, 63, 84, 89, 95, 123, 144, 206, 210–11, 220, 251, 253–54, 264, 348–50, 372*
Crofter-Cottar Arrangements *350*
Crofters *22ff.*
Crofters' Commission *48, 113*
Crofter's Year *289*
Crofts *15ff.*
    Number of crofts in Tiree *147, 372*
Crops (see also Food) *145*

D

Digital Archive of Scottish Gaelic (DASG) *4*
Diagrams *65, 70–71*
Drugget (drogaid) (from Mary Ann Campbell) *378*
Droving
    Cattle-dealers – post WWI *252*
    Falkirk Tryst *209, 244, 245*
    John Tough *242*
Duke *19, 117, 121, 136, 214, 254, 275, 291*

E

East End Comparative Prosperity *349*
Eric's family
    Lily Cregeen & the girls *275, 249, 333*
Evictions [see also Clearances]
    Evictions from *42*

F

Factors, see also Bàillidh Mòr, *79, 98, 132, 149, 255, 260, 275, 291, 314, 316*
Farms, Farming
    Tom Barr, farming in Tiree *66, 113, 210, 241, 252*
    Baugh farm *20, 117*
    Berwick Farmer's Association *68*
    Burning the tangle *225*
    Cheese-making *210, 245*
    Common grazing *120, 145, 217, 254, 262, 312, 329*
    Drainage *146*
    Goats Grazing with Cattle *59*
    Hay work *9, 112, 212, 249, 251–57, 263, 268, 270, 282, 302, 334–35, 339, 341, 350, 359, 365*

Herd-boy *305*
Hilipol Farm *221, 333*
Lamb sales at Crossapol *355*
Plean Farm *242*
Potato land *22, 95, 125, 144, 225, 350*
Potato planting 108, *120*
Reaping "team" *289*
Seaweed *22, 95, 101–03, 120, 124–25, 144–45, 225, 289, 350, 366, 383*
Township herds *265*

Filming in Tiree *294, 333, 337, 359, 362–67*

Fishermen, Sailors & Boats, see also Ships
Boats *92, 233*
Fisherman's clothing *344*
Fishing *25, 63, 211*
Fishing from Port Bhiosta *233*
Fuadach *54, 105, 110, 114, 134, 280, 343*
Manx schooner *114*
Rock-fishing *63, 372*
Wreck of Manx boat *55*

Folklife Surveys *2*

Food [see also Crops] *95*
Barley *96, 120, 253, 278*
Butcher in Tiree *16*
Diet *278, 357*
Eggs *125*
Fish *16, 63–65, 90, 106, 276, 278, 303, 334*
Healthy food *276*
Potatoes *22–23, 35, 90, 96, 102, 108–09, 144–46, 206, 253, 258, 265, 276, 278, 290, 350*
Rye *240, 290*
Whelk-soup *90*

G

Gaelic *9ff.*
Gaelic in Perth *72*
Gaelic Saying *19*
"Goirtean" names *310*

Genealogy
Balephuil families *36, 109, 220, 263, 331–32*
John Maclean's Family *70*
MacEachnie family history *343*
Neil MacPhail Maternal Ancestors *376*
Neil MacPhail's family *352*

I

Informants
Archie an tuirneir *216, 217, 241, 249*
Caroline Black *107, 110, 266*
Capt. Brown *336*
John Brown *14, 26, 27, 35, 40, 51, 101, 116, 122, 215, 225, 257, 263–64, 270, 272, 274, 282, 287, 304, 325, 331, 356, 359, 361, 363, 368–71, 374–75*
Dolly Cameron *105, 139, 366*
Flora Campbell *272, 317, 370, 373*
Mary Anne Campbell *69, 229, 257, 337, 376-78*
Minister, Mr Forbes *360*
Donald Kennedy *222*
Hector Kennedy *14, 24ff.*
Calum MacDonald *39, 53, 110, 123, 134, 264, 282*
Donald MacDonald *30*
Jimmie MacDonald *52, 108, 112, 220, 302*
Isabel Macdonald Johnston *367*
Archie Mackechnie *76, 86*
Hugh MacKinnon *28–30, 47, 63, 141, 243, 299, 304, 326*
Chrissie & Margaret Maclean *88, 205, 210–11, 244*
Donald Maclean *100, 234, 236*
John Maclean *45, 59, 70, 71, 138, 212, 216, 237, 251, 255, 270, 335, 336, 365, 371*
Mona & Angus Maclean *305*
Hector MacNeill *14, 141, 243, 267*

Mary MacPhail *9, 21, 30, 40–42, 73, 100, 140, 149, 222, 237, 311, 335, 369, 377*
Neil MacPhail *213, 319, 326, 346, 348, 352, 373*
Miss Martin *77, 78*
Mrs Macdonald *61, 135*
John Munn *117*
Alasdair Sinclair *213, 257, 277, 357, 361, 367, 381*
Donald Sinclair *38, 57, 107, 111, 121, 133, 135, 231, 258–59, 262, 267, 269, 277,* 302, *307, 343, 374*

Interviewers
    Donald Mackenzie *21, 50, 205, 212, 240, 244*
    Maggie MacKay *99, 100, 110, 117, 122, 135, 140, 225, 270-78*
Irish Folklore Commission *2*

K

Kelp industry 101-02, 225

L

Land-League *83, 108, 121, 258, 262, 283, 358, 366*
Literacy *294, 297, 306, 338*

P

Photographs *12, 43, 58, 68, 94, 98, 100, 122, 210, 281, 311, 331, 341, 353, 355, 370, 371, 377*
Piping, Pipers
    Duke of Roxburgh's Farewell 214
    Good pipers, Tinkers 21
    John Macdonald "am piobaire mòr" *214*
    MacArthur pupil of a MacCrimmon piper in Skye *346*
    Pipe-tunes - John Macdonald *214*
    Piping session *213*
    The 79's Farewell to Gibraltar 214
Place-names
    Ardbheag *100*

Argyll *2, 3*
Auchterarder *5, 204*
Balemartin *11, 37, 41, 57, 106, 110, 113, 119, 127, 136, 137, 145, 149–50, 214, 264–67, 272, 279, 283, 304, 317, 330, 340, 370*
Balenoe *22, 60, 108, 121, 125, 137, 139, 229–30, 258, 265, 285, 302, 335, 339*
Balephetrish *9, 28, 30, 65–67, 99–100, 130–33, 137, 140–44, 151, 210, 222, 230, 237, 239, 241–42, 252–53, 311–12, 347, 377*
Balephuil *14, 22, 35–36, 39–42, 51, 53, 77, 101–02, 105, 107, 109–10, 114–15, 122–23, 126, 131, 133, 139–40, 149, 215, 220, 223, 235, 250–51, 260–63, 267–68, 277, 279–80, 285, 290, 299, 304–05, 320, 331–33, 341, 357–58, 365–66, 374*
Balevullin *10, 42, 62, 108, 118, 121, 136–37, 213, 217–18, 229–33, 249, 257–58, 292, 303, 312, 314–15, 329, 339–40, 345, 375, 377*
Balphetrish *99, 253, 347*
Barra *37, 54, 60, 104, 108, 235–36, 262, 299, 307, 344*
Barrapol *17, 37–38, 41–42, 102, 109, 120, 126–27, 131, 137, 151, 228–30, 238, 250, 254, 256, 258, 262, 265–66, 285, 304, 306, 308, 310, 312, 326, 335, 342–44, 357–58, 376, 381*
Berwick *67, 68, 99*
Canada *69, 78, 79, 115, 119, 126, 137, 299, 312, 316, 320, 330, 346, 352, 377*
Colonsay *220, 266*
Cornaig *31, 32, 40, 91, 92, 94, 130, 270, 294, 311, 320, 344, 367, 376*
Cornaigbeg *59, 61, 65, 68, 70–73, 89, 100, 138, 141, 149, 151, 212, 216, 223, 237, 239, 247, 249, 251, 254–55, 262, 270, 292, 299, 335–36, 344–45, 365,*

371, 376–77
Cornaigmore 42, 45, 219, 236, 239, 242, 246, 314, 318
Crossapol 62–63, 79, 239, 249, 253, 309, 313, 355
Dùn Vaul Beag 12, 34
Eaglesview 204
Glasgow 74, 79, 123, 125, 139, 207–08, 221, 231–32, 266, 286, 301–03, 313, 338–40, 377
Heanish 117, 313, 315, 328
Hilipol 57ff.
Hynish 26, 38, 42, 46, 52, 107, 112–13, 146, 213–15, 220, 229, 234, 259, 268, 276, 285, 302, 305–307, 341, 359, 371–72
Inveraray 84, 108, 120, 222, 275
Iona 74, 307
Islay 54, 56, 102, 114, 312
Jura 74, 86, 235, 250
Keills 76, 249
Kenavara 55, 120, 127, 305, 381, 383
Kenovay 10, 33, 108, 140, 143, 219ff.
Kilkenneth 52, 118, 138–41, 149, 151, 221, 250, 294, 304, 308, 314, 316, 328
Kilmoluag 27, 45, 62, 72, 100, 149, 219, 220, 228, 242, 249, 284, 286, 292, 301, 303, 315–16, 327–29, 343–45, 364, 369
Kintyre 338
Kirkapol 120, 129, 130, 136, 293, 319, 355
Kirkopol 317, 319, 323, 346, 348, 352, 373
Lochboisdale 321
Lochside 51, 114, 122, 139, 215, 266, 332
Mannal 42, 118, 216, 236, 280, 286, 305, 315, 326, 328, 363, 370
Mid-Argyll 76
Middleton 22, 35, 42, 101, 119, 121, 128, 151, 294, 342, 383
Milton 29–30, 39, 367
Minard 77, 79, 107, 109
Montreal (Canada) 78
Morvern 313
Moss 16, 102, 108, 119, 131, 139, 225, 242–43, 304, 313–15, 329, 343–44, 363, 365, 371, 373
Mull 43, 45, 74, 129, 142, 211, 218, 221, 223–46, 280, 287, 307, 320, 329, 338, 353, 379
Newmilns 88, 91, 205, 222, 244
Patagonia 324
Sandaig 21, 22, 23, 40, 101–02, 104, 109, 118, 122, 124, 135, 225, 236, 261, 292, 294, 304, 308, 311, 314, 327, 335, 344, 366
Scarinish 16, 33, 63, 92, 125–26, 129, 133, 136–37, 143, 147, 149, 151, 228, 230, 236, 249, 273, 291, 304–05, 320, 330–31, 334, 342–43, 347, 365, 371, 373, 376
Skipnish 118–19, 315, 328
Soroby 45–46, 78, 136, 139, 277, 322, 323, 345
Stirlingshire 91, 118
Tiree 7, 9, 15ff.
Tobermory 21, 118, 123, 295, 353
Vancouver 78, 277
Whitehouse 41, 65-66, 88-89, 94, 98, 106, 143-44, 206, 208, 211, 216-17, 222, 226, 238, 247, 250, 311, 328
Postponement of Marriage 351
Potato famine 219, 231, 232, 239, 240, 253, 283
am bliadhna a' dh'fhalbh am buntata 231, 298, 306, 366

R

Religion 35
Baptist Church Services 36, 58, 306, 333,

337, 359, 360, 361, 367
  Expulsion of the Catholics *36*
  Sermon house – tigh sermon mhic Fhearchair *318*
Runrig Tenancy *35*

S

School of Scottish Studies Archives
  Fieldwork recordings 17 passim
  Filming 21/8/76 – Baptism *359, 360*
  Filming 23/8/76 Hector Kennedy & John Brown *363*
  Filming 24/8/76 Balephuil & Moss *365*
  Fred Kent & his bro George & Ian Fraser filming crew *359*
  Recorded 2/8/76 – Hector Kennedy *67, 138, 146, 239, 240, 241*
  Recorded 2/8/76 – JBrown – Tom Barr *66*
  Recorded 2/8/76 – John MacLean *67, 138, 146, 239, 240, 241*
  Recorded 5/8/76 – Hector Kennedy *235, 236, 334*
  Recorded 6/5/75 – Hector Kennedy *315, 317*
  Recorded 14/7/77 – Chrissie & Margaret Maclean *245, 247, 248*
  Recorded 14/08/76 – Angus Maclean *126*
  Recorded 16/6/75 – Hector Kennedy *17, 25, 89*
  Recorded 16/8/76 & 17/8/76 – Hector Kennedy *317*
  Recorded 19/8/76 – Hector Kennedy *341*
  Recorded 25/3/75 – Alasdair Sinclair *357*
  Recorded 25/8/76 – Donald Maclean *101, 226*
  Recorded 25/8/76 – John Brown *101, 226*
  Recorded 26/11/75 – Calum MacDonald *134*
  Recorded 30/11/75 – Mona & Angus Maclean *305*
  Recorded 1975/06 – Hector Kennedy *19*
  Recorded 1975/11/26 – Hector Kennedy *108*
  Recorded 1975/11/27 – Jimmie MacDonald *112*
  Recorded 1975/11/28 – Hector Kennedy *118*
  Recorded – Maclean sisters *210*
  Recorded on 18/8/76 – Mary Anne Campbell *229*
  SA1975/89 – Chrissie & Margaret Maclean *89*
  SA1976/14 – Chrissie & Margaret MacLean *205*
  SA1976/114 – Chrissie & Margaret MacLean *206*
  SA1976/115 – Chrissie & Margaret Maclean *244*
  SA1976/116 -137 – Tiree Field trip *249*
  SA1976/116 – Hector Kennedy *249, 250*
  SA1976/120 – John Brown *283*
  SA1979/81 – Chrissie & Margaret Maclean *246, 247*
  To be recorded *136, 219*
Sheiling *285*
Shepherds *42, 118, 221, 222, 227, 229, 235, 249, 250*
Shinty *115*
Ship, Boats
  Dunara Castle *331, 338*
  The Hebrides *338*
  The Marie Sterwart *331*
  The Sturdy, warship *83*
Songs, Singing
  'A nighean donn a Chornaig' *243*
  'Calum Beag' *274*
  'Dileab a' Chròig' *56*
  'Hog-is-hoireann Cul ri Comann a'

Bhàillidh' 41
'Ho-ro a' bhais an tèid thu lathair - Na tèid thu idir air ?ann choir'. 60
Iain MacLachlan na-h-Urvaig 299
Lullaby: 'Ba, ba, ba, mo leanabh' 373
Lullaby: 'Horan o's horan e' 373
'Maighstir sgoil nan duilleagan' 235
'Oran na Norwegian' 27
'Praise to Tobacco' 32
'San Gleann san Robh mi Òg' 46
Satire of miller at Cornaig 32
Song about Sunipol Campbells 142
Song by MacLachlan of Rahoy 237
Song of John Brown about a cartwright 27
Songs of Willie MacPhail 32, 40, 43, 44
Song to Mary Campbell in Tiree 345
Song to Tea 26
'Tha mi an seo gun chroit, gun sgoth' 26
Tiree bards by Hector Cameron 26, 31, 33, 279
'Tir nam beann, nam gleann 's nan breacan' 221
Willie MacPhail's songs 43
Storytelling, Story
Anecdote about Gregorson Campbell 345
Anecdote of body-snatchers 46
Anecdotes 17, 21, 26, 27, 32, 41, 46, 86, 91, 104, 118, 208, 209, 261, 293, 297, 305, 338, 345, 363, 372, 381
Battle of the Sheaves 51, 52
Stories of Land League 83
Story about Niceal – the witch 344
Story in Cape Breton 336
Story of Diarmad & Finn 38
Story of the warship Sturdy 83
Story of the last man to be hanged 131
Story of the man carrying a pig of whisky 115
Supernatural
Death Omen 369

Fairy Woman 128
Poltergeist 33
Premonitions of death 86
Second sight 308, 309
Superstitious Beliefs
Bad luck 9, 49, 288, 311
Ball of red thread 236, 262
Evil eye 91
Lucky & Unlucky Days 61, 97, 372
Lucky & unlucky months to marry 213
Places avoided after dark 130
Protective charms 288
Unlucky family & houses 39, 49, 62
Witches 118, 119, 132, 219, 235, 236, 261, 262, 344, 381

T

Thatched houses 22–23, 101, 105, 206, 228, 256, 289, 368
Tea-making 26
Tinkers, Travelling people in Tiree 20-21
Tiree Donated a bi-plane in WWI 325
Traditional Customs
Celebrating Christmas, New Year & Halloween 16
The Crofter's Years 289
First day of ploughing 245
Funeral Customs 10
Funeral invitations 10, 18, 37, 293
Funeral of Domhnull Chaluim Bàin 38
Funerals 10, 18, 37–39, 57, 73, 120, 122, 130, 136, 210, 267, 284, 293–95, 299, 304, 307, 322–26
Hallowe'en 245, 288
Harvest maiden 134, 245
Hilipol Traditions 354
Maighdean bhuana 110, 245
New Year hospitality 120
New Year's Day 62, 251, 289
Old New Year 352
Traditional care for elderly parents 351

    Wakes *134, 210, 259, 294, 295, 324*
Tunes
    'The 79's Farewell to Gibraltar' 214
    'The Duke of Roxburgh's Farewell' 214

W

War
    Peninsular War *347*
    Waterloo *207, 376, 381*
    World War I *19, 93, 113, 147, 252*
    World War II *113, 339*
Weather lore *282*
Weaving
    Patterrn for drugget 377-78
Whisky *3, 10, 19, 104, 115, 122, 208, 235, 259, 295, 321, 322, 323, 326, 336, 357*
    Petition against whisky at Funerals *322*
Writers
    Margaret Bennett *3, 5, 6*
    James Hunter [new book on crofting] *255*
    Martin MacGregor *3*
    Seán Ó Súilleabháin *2*
    T. C. Smout *3*

INDEX VOLUME 9
1977-1982

A

Animals
    Cattle, cows 14ff
    Cattle, de-horned 59
    Horses 58–59, 62, 81, 214, 268, 282, 325, 328, 368, 379, 416
    Sheep 14, 58-59, 63, 137, 185, 201, 207, 214, 224, 230, 272, 3231, 372, 391, 409
Ardnamurchan estate 186, 191

B

Baillidh Mòr 29, 32, 76–77, 131–32, 266, 359
Bards 14, 20, 40, 94, 123, 129, 131, 306, 353, 367, 384, 419, 432
Byre 23, 28–29, 50–52, 110–12, 205, 274, 375

C

Census 309, 313, 356, 394
Clearances 11ff,
    Achateny 199
    Ben Shiant 187, 466
    Hilipol 54
    Mannal 11, 17, 69, 290, 357
    Ross 226
    'The Clearances' – STV film 443
Coal merchant 114
Cottars 245, 452
Crofter earnings 107
Crofters 10–11, 17, 18, 53, 61–62, 71, 77, 90–91, 100–03, 116, 126, 176, 182, 196, 214, 236, 245, 259, 266, 272, 289–93, 305, 309ff.
Decline of crofters 416
Crofts 14, 17, 19ff.
Cures
    Mary Kennedy 298, 300
    Donald Sinclair 297

D

Digital Archive of Scottish Gaelic (DASG) 4
Decay of a community 354
Decline of Kilmoluag 56
Diagrams 28, 34, 51, 115, 145, 195, 199, 205, 246–47
Dykes 29, 33, 74, 76–77, 183, 198, 200, 202, 206, 209, 216, 239, 249, 257–61, 267–75, 300, 305, 368, 372, 423, 428, 479

E

Eric, Illness (1980,1981) 333, 367
Evictions [see Clearances]
    John Campbell 54
    Jn MacColl 183
    MacDiarmid 324

F

Factors [see Baillidh Mòr, Clearances, Evictions]
Farms, Farming
    Common grazing 59, 186, 209, 245, 272, 351, 354, 414–15
    Herd boy 63, 94
    Lazy-beds 33, 188, 192, 271, 406, 416, 447
    Loading Tangles 288
    Mingary farm 187
    Plough-team 59, 61, 416
    Seaweed 60, 103, 273, 277, 289, 321–22, 340, 394, 410, 416, 423, 434, 449, 450; Tangle 288–89
Farm Implements
    Cas-chrom 416, 428, 447
    Coran (Sickle) 429
    Flail 25
Fencibles 264, 426
Film – The Clearances documentary:
    Interviewers, informants, filming locations

    & facts *446*
    Moira Allison (film researcher) *455, 462*
    Angus Henderson (Ben Shiant Clearance) *466, 481, 484*
    Aerial photo of cleared of Bourblaig *463*
    Calum Beaton (informal ceilidh) *457*
    Patrick Boyle (film producer) *446*
    Roy Campbell (University of Stirling) *471, 472*
    Capt A. Fraser (Uig, Skye) *469*
    Castle at Carnasserie *446*
    Ceilidh at Herbusta (Skye) *457*
    Clearance of Glenconon (Skye) *469*
    Dukes of Argyll (clearance) *468*
    Bob Duncan *455, 463*
    Eric - Documentary adviser & co-writer *446*
    Frigate Hercules *451*
    Gaelic service *465*
    Charles Gillies *456, 457*
    Malcolm Gillies *456*
    James Hunter (historian) *470*
    Roddy Johnson (harvesting seaweed) *449*
    Kintail clearances (A. Macleod) *469*
    Loch & Sellar (factors) *459*
    Donald Angus Macdonald *448*
    Jonathan Macdonald *461*
    Roderick Macdonald *453*
    Dond Mackay *450, 453*
    Fulton Mackay (presenter) *446, 461–63, 470*
    Alasdair Macleod (Glenconon, Skye) *469*
    Donald Macleod (Syre) *458*
    Sir Iain Moncreiffe *471*
    Musical on the clearances by Elliot Rude (Bettyhill) *460*
    Father Antony Ross (Lord Rector, Edinburgh University) *471*
    Seaweed cutting *449*
    Seaweed factory *423, 450*
    Patrick Sellar (factor) *459*
    Story of Alasdair Mòr *451*

Fishermen, Sailors & Boats
    Carbhanach *29, 30*
    Tiree fishermen *42*
    Wrecks *374*

Food
    Edible seaweeds *321, 340*
    Limpets & whelks *340, 429*

G

Gaelic *14, 72ff.*
Gaelic Phrases *339*
Genealogy
    Barrapol Families *266*
    Brown family Mannal *302*
    Campbells *263ff.*
    The Cooper *258, 285, 309, 385, 405, 426*
    Lamont Family History *292*
    MacDonald family tree *115*
    MacLean Family Tree *145, 349, 388*
    Hugh MacLeans Forebears & Family *314*

I

Informants
    John Brown *18, 53, 65, 67, 94, 105, 123, 129, 137, 261, 303, 343, 361, 367, 372, 398, 401, 412–13, 430*
    Lachie & Mary Cameron *125*
    Archie Campbell *182, 185, 191–193, 209, 265, 363*
    Flora Campbell –Florie a' Bhaird *14, 129, 280, 333, 353, 371, 381, 400, 411, 418*
    Colin Fletcher *225, 229, 474–78*
    Angus Henderson *29, 182, 226, 466, 475, 481, 484*
    Hector Kennedy *10, 14, 26–27, 49, 54, 62, 65, 70, 73–77, 87, 90, 95, 123, 133, 258, 260, 265–69, 282, 303, 332, 340, 344, 347, 360–63, 367, 373, 384–85, 394–95, 406, 418, 423, 428–29*
    Mary Kennedy *9, 57, 68, 97, 298, 300,*

    333
    Sandy Kennedy *22–23, 71*
    John Lamont *28, 38, 45, 58, 66, 99, 102, 289, 290, 293, 352, 357, 368*
    Alasdair MacDonald *50, 90–91, 110, 117, 124, 134, 275, 286, 289, 291, 294, 335, 343, 372, 375, 407, 415, 422*
    Murdoch Macdonald *57, 95–96, 117*
    Hugh MacEachern *116, 135, 175*
    Donald & Tina Macfarlane *474*
    Hugh Mackenzie *189–90, 194, 214*
    Hugh Mackinnon *14, 21, 30*
    Malcolm Mackinnon *92, 111–12, 120*
    Sandy Mackinnon *432*
    Alec Maclean *93, 276, 382, 385, 406, 420, 429*
    Alec Hector Maclean *421*
    Chrissie Maclean *328, 386, 434*
    Chrissie & Margaret Maclean *78, 84, 142, 315, 321*
    Hugh MacLean *258, 262, 266–79, 282, 288, 308, 312, 336, 344, 361–64, 382, 394, 401, 406, 422, 424*
    John Maclean *24, 56, 58, 93ff.*
    Lachie Maclean *93, 217, 229, 373, 462, 477*
    Neill Alex Maclean *393*
    Morag Macleod *476*
    Alasdair MacNeil *46, 259*
    Hector & Flora MacPhail *70, 73, 273, 332, 374*
    Hector Meek *261, 393*
    Donald Morrison *478, 482, 485*
    Mary Morrison *476, 485*
    Donald Sinclair *9–10, 65, 104, 258, 267, 285, 295, 300, 304, 309, 407, 412, 478*
Interviewers
    Anne-Berit Borchgrevink *257, 262, 269, 270, 274*
    Patrick Boyle *281, 446*

    John MacInnes *311*
    Justus Wamikoya and Luke Wanjaa (Kenyan students) *481*
    Maggie Mackay *9, 16, 40, 72, 76, 87ff*
    Donald Mackenzie *78, 84, 142, 315, 321, 386, 434, 474*

L

Lamonts in Canada *432*
Land League *70, 103, 215, 243, 305, 410, 433*
Land raid
    Balephetrish *44, 70, 290*
Lord MacDonald *267, 282, 284, 319, 367, 395*

M

MacArthur of Sanday *263*
MacArthurs *18–22, 30, 74, 263–64, 268, 284, 309–10, 346, 349, 363–64, 381–82, 403–04, 407, 424, 429, 465*
Manx *334*
Maori *198, 250*
Medicines, see Cures
Morlanachd *267, 300, 305*
Murchanaich, descendants of a Murchadh Campbell *312ff*

N

Nicknames *384*
Jimmie Norris, The tinsmith *74*
    Paraffin lamps in Tiree *50, 74*

P

Peat-cutting *447*
Photographs *36, 70–71, 75, 86, 111, 120, 124, 129, 140, 210, 269, 288, 315–16, 320, 357, 367, 372, 386, 391, 413, 469, 486*
Place-names
    Achosruch *210*
    Alberta (Canada) *291*

Ardnamurchan *147, 182–86, 191, 197, 202, 210, 215, 443–46, 462*
Argyll *20, 52, 87, 263, 331, 343, 350, 443–46, 463, 468–70, 479*
Australia *189, 291, 369, 432*
Ayrshire *142*
Balemartin, B'martin *11, 14, 18–19, 30, 69, 94, 109, 114, 129–31, 282, 290–92, 306, 309, 338, 346, 353–54, 368, 381, 396, 400-01, 406, 414, 418–19, 422*
Balenoe *29, 39, 124, 263, 282–84, 290, 312–13, 336–37, 340–41, 345–47, 365, 401, 407*
Balephetrish *9, 13, 21, 39, 44, 70, 86–87, 92, 95, 217, 257, 275–76, 258, 281, 285, 290, 323–25, 357, 371–73, 387, 397, 411, 422*
Balephuil *21, 58, 69, 125, 135, 259, 263, 273, 282–87, 304, 306, 309–14, 333, 337–38, 346, 349–51, 361, 368–69, 372, 384, 390–91, 396–400, 404, 407, 409, 414, 422, 424, 429*
Baleview *268, 272, 282, 285, 304*
Balevullin *9, 23, 41–43, 46, 49, 54, 73, 77, 96, 111, 116, 120, 135, 143, 285, 297, 313, 320–24, 372, 396, 417, 422, 432*
Barra *49, 325, 365, 372*
Barrapol *32, 35, 109, 258ff.*
Beinn Hough *53–54, 110, 282, 324, 342, 350–51*
Benbecula *427*
Ben Hough *286, 331, 367, 372*
Ben Hynish *260–61*
Ben Shiant *183, 187, 194, 204, 207, 209, 463, 466*
California (USA) *264*
Canada *73, 105, 109, 122, 188, 281, 291, 293, 304, 306, 309–10, 318, 349, 368, 373, 432*
Caolas *314, 349–50, 372, 378, 380, 384–85, 405, 424–26*
Carnasserie Castle *463*
Castle Tioram *463*
Clunary *469*
Cnoc Bhiosda *49, 56, 92, 120, 284, 378*
Cornaig *12, 39, 41, 63, 143, 293, 306, 416, 419*
Cornaigbeg *57, 81, 116, 125, 132, 139, 140, 217, 236, 238, 239, 276-77, 313, 343, 385, 387, 420*
Cornaigmore *11, 24–25, 41, 73, 76, 82, 96–97, 113, 124, 238, 266, 286, 315–16, 421, 428*
Croish *38, 39, 40–41, 55, 58, 66, 74, 90, 99–102, 117–18, 121, 289–91, 352, 357–58*
Crossapol *55, 67, 325, 333–34, 399, 432*
Dervaig *227, 476, 485*
Duirinish *464*
Dumbarton *47*
Firth of Lorne *463*
Galtrigill *464*
Glen Cannell *462*
Gott *13, 54, 93, 258, 270, 275, 288, 341, 378, 422*
Greenhill *27, 30, 32, 35, 41, 55, 72, 100, 269, 275, 291, 342, 366, 394, 410, 422, 426*
Grigadale *188, 189*
Herbusta *457*
Hilipol *29, 32, 54, 72, 76–77, 83, 87, 94–95, 126, 257ff.*
Hough *53–54, 74ff.*
Howmore, S. Uist *450, 453*
Hynish *9, 12, 46, 69, 105, 137, 177, 260–61, 292, 296–98, 304–06, 350, 362, 369, 382, 391, 409, 412, 422*
Inveraray *130, 199, 262, 368, 378, 398, 467–68, 479*
Iona *267, 475, 479, 483–84*
Islay *479*

Kenavara *268, 270–72, 275, 277, 372*
Kenovay *22, 60, 66, 113, 283, 285, 323, 365, 373, 387, 422, 436*
Kentra *474*
Kilchoan *182, 184, 189–91, 209, 237–39, 242, 362, 373, 466*
Kilkenneth *11, 30–33, 41, 72, 89, 94, 263, 269, 276, 305, 307–08, 338, 341, 358, 364, 382, 393, 404, 417, 422–25, 432*
Kilmoluag *9, 11, 40ff.*
Kirkapol *43, 272, 292, 323, 363, 414, 421*
Lairg *458, 461*
Langais *448*
Lismore *264, 391, 394*
Loch Bharrapol *423, 425*
Loch Carnan, S. Uist *447*
Loch Euport *448*
Lochmaddy *447–50, 453*
Lorgill *464*
Luing *53*
Malaclete *451*
Manitoba *264, 312–14, 336, 346, 361, 397*
Mannal *11, 15, 17, 28ff.*
Mid-Argyll *52, 443, 445–46, 463*
Middleton *24, 31, 35, 74, 263, 266, 308, 360, 404, 422, 424, 429*
Mingary *183, 187, 209, 221, 244*
Moidart *199, 466*
Morvern *117, 197, 462, 470*
Moss *14, 21–33, 69–74, 121, 248, 259, 263, 287, 305–10, 364, 370, 382, 404, 407, 411, 419, 428–30, 433*
Mull *23, 26, 52, 81, 113, 143, 147ff.*
Newmilns *78, 84, 142, 315, 321, 386, 414, 434*
New Zealand *198, 216*
Oban *13, 59, 70, 108–09, 139, 210, 257, 280, 328, 331, 389, 391, 447, 452, 462, 481*
Ormsaig *209*
Penimore *476*
Port Bhiosda *52, 56*
Portree *218, 454*
Salen *215, 225, 229, 264, 265, 309, 425, 474, 477, 481, 485*
Sandaig *74, 259, 268–69, 311, 346, 361, 384, 395*
Sandaig boundary *74*
Sanday *263, 309, 350, 422*
Sassenachs *226*
Scarinish *30, 47, 65, 121, 233, 280, 302, 310, 353, 388, 408, 417, 430–31*
Skye *147, 215, 218–19, 228, 270, 357, 443–47, 466, 469–70, 476–77, 485*
Snishval *450*
Sollas *448, 451, 453*
Soroby *302, 323, 337, 347*
Staffin district *456*
Stoneybridge *449, 453*
Strathaven *434*
Strathnaver *458*
Strontian *210*
Sutherland *443–46, 458, 460*
Tayvallich *215*
Tiree *7ff.*
Tobermory *23, 31, 182, 185, 226–27, 324, 337, 402, 408–09, 436, 466, 475–76, 481, 484*
Tolsta *406*
Trotternish *447*
Uig *447, 454, 465, 469*
Uist *277, 443–50*
Ulva *26, 225, 475, 485–86*
Vaul *261, 275, 307, 353, 356*
Plants, wild flowers
    Seilisdearan [Iris] *29*
Potato famine *318, 451*
    am blaidhna a' dh'fhalbh am buntata *72, 123, 292*

Potato ground *18, 81, 176*
Prince Charles Edward Stewart, memories *199*

R

Raid, see Land raid
Religion
    Preaching house *76, 83, 257*
Runrig *414*

S

School of Scottish Studies Archives
    Filming Ishbel singing Tiree *281*
    Recorded 2/3/82 – Alasdair MacDonald *375*
    Recorded 3/12/80 – Hector Kennedy *340*
    Recorded 8/12/80 – Hector Kennedy *363*
    Recorded 8/12/80 – John Brown *361*
    Recorded 9/7/82 – Mcfadyen *84, 304, 317, 321, 340, 418, 483*
    Recorded 17/5/82 Hugh Maclean *282, 303, 321, 401, 483*
    Recorded 19/4/82 – Chrissie Maclean *386*
    Recorded 19/5/82 – John Brown *412*
    Recorded 20/5/82 – Alasdair MacDonald *415*
    Recorded 21/5/82 – Hector Kennedy *407, 418*
    Recorded 22/3/82 – Hugh Maclean *258, 262, 266, 268, 270, 279, 282, 288, 308, 312, 336, 344, 361, 362, 364, 382, 394, 401, 406, 422, 424*
    Recorded 23/4/82 – Hector Kennedy *395*
    Recorded 23/5/82 – Hector Kennedy *428*
    Recorded 23/11/77 – Alasdair Macdonald *53, 55, 102*
    Recorded 24/11/77 – John brown *105*
    Recorded 24/11/77 – John Brown *67*
    Recorded 10/7/82 – Mary Morrison *486*
    Recorded tape 1977/78 – Chrissie & Margaret MacLean *80*
    SA1974/228 & 229 – Hector Kennedy *269*
    SA1977/171 – Chrissie & Margaret Maclean *84*
    SA1977/172 – Chrissie & Margaret Maclean *85*
    SA1978/46 – Chrissie & Margaret Maclean *142*
    SA1979/74 – Hector Kennedy *285*
    SA 1979/75 – Hector Kennedy *286*
    SA1979/76 – Alasdair Macdonald *300*
    SA 1979/77 – Hector Macdougall *290*
    SA1979/78 – Hector Kennedy *304*
    SA1979/79 – Hector Kennedy *306*
    SA 1979/80 – Hugh Maclean *308*
    SA1979/81 – Chrissie & Margaret Maclean *317*
    SA1979/82 – Chrissie & Margaret Maclean *319*
    SA1980/110 – John Lamont *357*
    SA1980/113 – Hugh Maclean *364*
    SA1982/93 – Hugh Maclean *402*
    SA1982 – Chrissie Maclean 24/6/82 *434*
    Tape 21/4/1980 – Chrissie & Margaret Maclean *222, 317, 321, 328, 418*
    Topics to be Recorded *310*
    Visit 2/12/80 – Hugh Maclean *336*
    Visit 15/5/82 – Neill Alex Maclean *393*
    Visit 16/5/82 – Neil & Ellen Kennedy *396*
    Visit 18/5/82 – Hector Kennedy *406*
    Visit 22/3/82 Flora Campbell *381*
Settlers at Kilmoluag *377, 378*
Shieling huts *77, 208, 212, 257, 274*
Donald Sinclair, life
    Father's funeral *300*
    Gift of healing *297*
    Loss of his father in childhood   *296*
    Prisoner-of-war *295*
    Quarry worker, highly skilled

Songs, Singing
    'An caoidh a' mhisgte' *404*
    'A nighean donn a' Chornaig' *83*
    'An teid thu leam a'Mhaggi Chailein' by High MacDonald *11, 30*
    Balephetrish raid Verse *44, 290*
    Elegy by Angus Maclean *125*
    Hector MacDougall song *45*
    'M'fheudail, a' chas a shuil air fad' *344*
    'Mo nighean donn a'Chornaig' *21*
    'Neill Mac Bhannchaidh Bhain' *410*
    Poem about Crimean war by Wm Livingstone *425*
    Song about the Crimean War *344*
    Song of Willie MacPhail *119*
    Song of W. MacPhail *340*
    Songs *21, 22, 44, 45, 95, 220, 229, 281, 306, 334, 358, 374, 430, 477, 485*
    Songs of Alasdair Sinclair *21*
    Verse on the MacCualrigs *311*
St Kildan called MacQueen *276*
Storytelling, Story
    Account of wreck of a Swedish boat *328*
    Anecdote about a wreck *324*
    Anecdote about bogha (buoy) Ailain Uasail *364*
    Anecdotes *19, 31, 81, 85–86, 88, 103, 131, 186, 189, 197, 215, 263, 266, 285, 305, 309, 324–25, 328, 358, 361, 364, 383, 418, 430, 477*
    Story *20, 25, 43, 90, 117–18, 122, 194, 224, 250, 264, 270–71, 290, 299–300, 311, 316, 344, 367, 374, 457, 475*
    Story about a man named Clerk at Kilmoluag *118*
    Story about about 'the Currier', fight *43, 90, 117-118, 122*
    Story of Alasdair Mòr *451*
    Story of the last man to be hanged *25*
    Story-teller *90, 194, 299, 475*

STV (see also Film – The Clearances documentary) *443, 445, 446*
Supernatural
    Fairy woman *412, 425*
    Second sight *125–26, 345*
    Water horses *282, 286*
    Wraith *127*
Superstitious Beliefs
    Evil eye *68, 320, 399, 412*
    Lucky & unlucky days *126*
    Superstition *278*
    Unlucky families *279, 307*

T

Tacksmen *221, 394, 424*
Thatched Houses *23, 24, 40, 43, 50–52, 61, 71, 74, 91, 112, 120–21, 196, 201, 210, 212, 225, 249, 283, 284, 292, 376, 406-07, 448*
    Rye straw *24*
Tilly lamp *294*
Traditional Customs
    Burials 323, *348*
    Christmas & New Year celebrations *434*
    Coffins *114*
    Coffins covered with soot *348, 402*
    Funeral Invitations *384, 387, 402, 417, 436*
    Funerals *31, 144, 222, 285, 319, 337, 345, 347, 421, 436*
    Old New Year [January 13th] *137*
    Rowan tree, planting near house *9, 10*
    Wakes *107, 319*
    Weddings *325*
Traditional house *375*

W

Wars
    Crimean War *344, 404*
    Peninsular War *38, 357*
    Waterloo *134, 286*

Whisky *22–23, 68–69, 87, 111, 118, 187,*
303, 321–22, 408–09, 418, 422, 430, 436,
476, 483
  Drams *141, 339, 374, 384, 430*
  Sacanach *23, 30*
  Whisky at Funerals *31*
Duncan MacGregor Whyte Paintings *232,*
389–91, 398, 412, 414
Writers
  Margaret Bennett *3, 5, 6*
  Martin MacGregor *3*
  Seán Ó Súilleabháin *2*
  T. C. Smout *3*

APPENDIX A

"The Life and Legacy of Eric R. Cregeen"

(This essay opens each of the nine volumes)

This volume is part of a project inspired by the work of one of the most influential oral historians of the 20th century, Eric Radcliffe Cregeen (1921–83). He recorded people from many walks of life and made major contributions to the Manx Language and Folklife Surveys; the Royal Commission on the Ancient and Historical Monuments of Scotland, and to the Archives of the School of Scottish Studies (Special Collections at the University of Edinburgh). Meticulous in his methodology, Cregeen kept detailed fieldwork journals, which he anticipated using for further research and in preparation of publications. Sadly that was not to be, as he died in 1983 at the age of 61.

    While most of the tape-recordings were made in Scotland, Cregeen's roots were in the Isle of Man. He did not grow up there but was born in Dewsbury, Yorkshire, where his father was a Methodist clergyman. However, both parents were Manx; his mother's people, the Radcliffes, were from Peel, where his grandfather had a smiddy, and his father's family were from the south of the island.

    Throughout childhood and adolescence, Eric and his siblings spent school holidays on the island, "at home" among their own people. During these formative years Eric developed a passion for the Manx language, social history and culture, and he began to write down information gleaned from local folk, particularly the older generation, and to make lists of Manx vocabulary.

    In 1935, he won a scholarship to the Leys School, Cambridge, and in 1939 went on to university. He studied History and Latin at Christ's College and became an avid reader of Anthropology. With academic rigour he could combine all these disciplines while drawing from his own experience to practise and perfect the skills of an oral historian. His studies were interrupted by the war, however, and Eric (a conscientious objector) worked on farms.

    After the war he resumed university and during the holidays headed for the Isle of Man. As his journal of 1948 shows, ties to the island seemed stronger than ever:

> April 1:
>
> I walked along the quay and the shore road - black, cold night, pierced by a few stars, a brilliant planet, the light of the lighthouse and a few blueish lamps along the quay. The sea was thudding heavily on the shore – I cdnt. see it in the blackness. There wasn't a person on the streets, but I felt as I walked that I was at home. Here my forebears farmed and fished, wrought iron and built houses, lived and died obscure but known in a small community. Here a man meant something. Here people live close to elemental things - winds, earth, the sea - and they become themselves elemental and simple and eternal by sharing in this life.

During the university holidays Eric volunteered to assist with the Manx Language Survey that had been set up by Museum Director, William Cubbin. Inspired by the work of the Irish Folklore Commission, Cubbin made sure that all volunteers received training, based on Seán Ó Súilleabháin's classic guide for fieldworkers, *A Handbook of Irish Folklore* (Dublin, 1942):

> Information should be written down fully (and, where possible, in the actual words used) as soon as possible after obtaining it, if not at the time...Plans or rough sketches are valuable aids to verbal descriptions of implements or buildings, etc.

In 1948, the Irish Folklore Commission sent a special van to the island, driven by folklore collector Kevin Danaher, who had developed a built-in recording studio. Eric was among the volunteer collectors who helped record the voices of Manx speakers, which Danaher cut on 12-inch discs and deposited in the Archives of the Irish Folklore Commission. Copies were also placed in the Archives of Manx Museum, adding to the wax cylinder recordings made in the 1920s by Norwegian linguist Carl Marstrander.

When his last exam at Cambridge was over, Eric returned to the island and to the work he loved: August 13, 1948 "At Manx Museum; classified 24 Manx notebooks..." In September he applied for the post as Secretary and Assistant Director of the Manx Museum and on October 1, 1948 he wrote: "Began work in the Manx Museum .... Basil Megaw is a kindly chief ...."

In his new role, he implemented the Museum's plan for a Manx Folklife Survey to help "build up a picture of Manx traditional life as it survived fifty years ago, and earlier...." Collectors made every effort "to gather a mass of unrecorded information about buildings, crafts, tools and utensils, agriculture and fishing, dress and ornament, customs and beliefs, together with details of the people then alive and incidents in their life."

Cregeen remained in the post until 1950, after which he became a schoolmaster. In 1954, when an opportunity arose to re-engage with his love of oral history and folklife, he took up a post as Resident Tutor in Argyll for Glasgow University's Extra-Mural Department. As well as breaking new ground in adult education, he soon began to explore the Gaelic traditions of Argyllshire, finding strong similarities to his experiences on the Isle of Man. Again he felt at home among people who lived off the land and sea, and whose knowledge, skills and wisdom sustained their lifestyle and their culture. The evening classes in rural communities drew together folk from all walks of life, gave rise to lively discussions, and, for Cregeen, opportunities to continue fieldwork. His journals, tape-recordings and photographs during these years record a way of life that will never be seen again.

From 1964 to '65 Cregeen had a year's sabbatical when he received a Nuffield award to study Social History and Social Anthropology at Cambridge. He had already made an impressive contribution to the Archives of the School of Scottish Studies when, in 1966, he was appointed by the University of Edinburgh as Lecturer in Scottish Studies. With energy, enthusiasm and dedication he continued his research and fieldwork recording, regularly following up with lectures and publications.

The 1970s saw an increasing interest in oral history in Britain, and in 1973, under the leadership of Paul Thompson (University of Essex), a group of eminent scholars founded the Oral History Society. The following year Cregeen joined a prestigious group of conference speakers that now reads as a Who's Who of Oral History: Charles Parker (pioneer of the BBC's oral history programmes), Seán Ó Súilleabháin (Irish Folklore Commission), Christopher Smout (Scottish historian), George Ewart Evans (Suffolk folklorist), Robin Page Arnot (founder of Labour Research Department, University of Wales) as well as Alan Bruford and John MacQueen (School of Scottish Studies). The collective aim, summed up by Cregeen, was that the oral historian should primarily be concerned with "those sections of society which are unlikely to leave behind them any quantity of memoirs, diaries, or correspondence from which history can subsequently be written."

In 1978, Cregeen co-founded The Scottish History Group, delivering an opening address that now seems prophetic: "the recordings we make now will be a powerful aid to future generations living in a much-changed society." He could not have foreseen just how changed society would be, or that we would have technology that allows world-wide access to recordings – over 2,000 tracks of Cregeen's recordings (approximately 10%), are online via Tobar an Dualchais/Kist o Riches. The hand-written fieldwork journals that inform the recordings have not been accessible until now, as they have remained with Lily Cregeen, who accompanied her husband on several fieldtrips to Argyll and the Outer Hebrides.

Writing in 2001, Professor T. C. Smout, Historiographer Royal of Scotland, described Cregeen as "a social scientist of the highest order... a very fine historian and a very fine anthropologist... far in advance of his time ... no one since has put the two disciplines together so effectively to illuminate the life of the Highlands." And in 2016, during his keynote address welcoming an international audience of Celtic scholars, Dr Martin MacGregor of the University of Glasgow concluded: "Eric Cregeen was one of the most significant cultural scholars to have worked in Scotland in the last 50 years... innovative and inspirational, his fieldwork is remarkable for its quantity and quality."

Scotland, and folklorists globally, owe a huge debt of gratitude to Eric Cregeen for the treasure-trove of recordings, photographs and journals he left, documenting the lives and traditions of crofters, fishermen, housewives, shepherds, cattle-dealers, drovers, blacksmiths, horse-dealers, carpenters, tradespeople, weavers, craftspeople, children, healers, whisky-makers, teachers and clergy. It is only fitting that we should remember him and look after his legacy in a way that he himself would have done had he had the opportunity. Eric Cregeen had great hopes of publishing much of the material he recorded and collected, and it is our hope that this project is a worthwhile contribution to achieving that purpose.

THE PROJECT

Mrs Lily Cregeen, custodian of her husband's journals, initiated this project with Grace Notes Scotland, a Scottish charity "dedicated to handing on tradition". Under the title 'The Cregeen Journals: Sustainability, Land-use, Language and Culture', the project has been led by folklorist Dr Margaret Bennett, former lecturer at the University of Edinburgh's School of Scottish Studies.

Eric R. Cregeen's journals, written between 1938 and 1982, kept a record of his ideas, travels, and fieldwork carried out in the Isle of Man and the West Highlands of Scotland. They include notes on local culture, social history, features of landscape and archaeology; his development of research methods; and accounts of visits made in the quest to document the way of life and traditions of people on the Isle of Man and the West Highlands who lived off the land and the sea.

As the journals collectively amount to almost 4,000 pages, it was essential to engage a team to digitize and transcribe them in order to conserve the collection for future generations and for further research. A bid to Heritage Lottery Fund secured 90% of the funding for the project, which was carried out over 20 months and, upon completion, achieved the following aims:

- Page by page digital images of the unpublished fieldwork journals.
- Scans of Cregeen's photograph collection.
- Typed transcriptions of the hand-written journals to prepare for a digital, searchable archive, accessible worldwide, to be hosted by the University of Edinburgh (Special Collections, School of Scottish Studies Archive).
- Visits to schools, oral history groups and community centres located in 14 communities where Cregeen worked, presenting oral history workshops, public events ('talks') and exhibitions of journals and photographs relevant to each community.
- Editing, typesetting and printing of all the journals, showing the original handwriting with a transcription of each page, bound in nine volumes.
- Donation of digital images to the University of Glasgow's Digital Archive of Scottish Gaelic (DASG, an online repository of digitised texts and lexical resources for Scottish Gaelic) with the purpose of adding Cregeen's diagrams, sketches and lists or notes on Gaelic terminology to their database.
- Exhibition and public lecture featuring Cregeen's life and work at the National Library of Scotland, Edinburgh.

NOTES ON METHODOLOGY

As the journals were originally for Eric Cregeen's own benefit, he used non-standard abbreviations, such as "mkg" (making) "gr'fr" (grandfather), to help him write at speed. A style sheet was devised, as a reference guide for transcribers, though it will become apparent that most transcribers found it easier to write the words out in full. Given the scope and time-frame of the project we abandoned an attempt to restore abbreviations and, as readers will discover, some other features of the originals. Where words could not be deciphered, question marks are inserted, and it is hoped users will make use of the Notes section so that corrections can be made. Many of the placenames are not on maps and, although we sought advice, there are several that require further research. Editing has been minimal, with deletions of small sections which seemed redundant, too personal, or confidential.

Several of the journals have an aide-memoire inserted by Lily Cregeen, noting key points, places and/or people featured in the journal. As these pages can still serve that purpose, Lily's notes are also transcribed.

Readers are reminded that these volumes are intended as a research tool for school projects and teacher resources; local history groups and individuals interested in days gone by; and for scholars conducting research.

Margaret Bennett
Grace Notes Scotland, Board of Trustees
Professor of the Royal Conservatoire of Scotland, Glasgow
Hon. Professor of Antiquities and Folklore, Royal Scottish Academy, Edinburgh
Honorary Research Fellow at the University of St Andrews.

APPENDIX B

Publications by Eric R. Cregeen

BOOKS

Cregeen, Eric R. (ed.) 1963 *Inhabitants of the Argyll Estate 1779*. Edinburgh: Scottish Record Society.

Cregeen, Eric R. (ed.) 1964 *Argyll Estate Instructions: Mull, Morven, Tiree, 1771—1805*. Edinburgh: Scottish History Society.

Cregeen, Eric R. and MacKenzie, Donald W. 1978 *Tiree Bards and their Bardachd*, Coll: Society of West Highland and Island Historical Research.

ARTICLES

Cregeen, Eric R. 1954 'Skeealyn Edard Karugher', Creneash (Manx fishing taboos), Coraa Ghailckagh, Isle of Man.

Cregeen, Eric R. 1954 'Extra-Mural Venture', *MacTalla,* Argyll Education Committee Teachers' Magazine, p. 8.

Cregeen, Eric R. and Cregeen, Sheila. 1955–62 Notes on fifty sites and finds in annual issues of *Discovery and Excavation Scotland*. [1955, 4 pp; 1956, 9 pp; 1957, 8 pp; 1958, 14 pp; 1958, 18 pp.]

Cregeen, Eric R. 1957 'Extra-Mural Classes in the West Highlands', *Scottish Adult Education,* Vol. 20, 6—10.

Cregeen, Eric R. 1959 'Recollections of an Argyllshire Drover' *Scottish Studies* Vol. 3 No. 2, 143-161.

Cregeen, Eric R. 1960 'In Partnership: Adult Education in the County of Argyll' *Scottish Adult Education,* Vol. 30, 16—21.

Cregeen, Eric R. 1965 'Flailing in Argyll' *Journal of the Society for Folk Life Studies*, (ed. J. Geriant Jenkins), Vol. 3, 90.

Cregeen, Eric R. 1967 'The Ducal House of Argyll', *Chambers' Encyclopaedia,* Oxford: Pergamon Press.

Cregeen, Eric R. 1968 'The Changing Role of the House of Argyll in the Scottish Highlands' in *History and Social Anthropology,* ASA Monograph 7, (ed. I. Lewis), London, 153-192.

Cregeen, Eric R. 1969 'The Tacksmen and their successors: a study of tenurial reorganisation in Mull, Morven and Tiree in the early 18th century' in *Scottish Studies* Vol. 13 No. 2, 92-144.

Cregeen, Eric R. 1974 'Oral Sources for The Social History of the Scottish Highlands and Islands' *Oral History* Vol. 2, No.2, 23-36.

Cregeen, Eric R. 1974 'Oral Tradition and Agrarian History in the West Highlands.' *Oral History,* Volume 2, No. 1, 15-33.

Cregeen, Eric R. 1974 'The Interview in Social History' *Oral History,* Vol. 2, No. 2, 1-4.

Cregeen, Eric R. 1974 'Oral Sources for the Social History of the Scottish Highlands and Islands', *Oral History,* Vol. 2, No. 2, 23-36.

Cregeen, Eric R. 1975 'Donald Sinclair', *Tocher* 18, 41-65.

Cregeen, Eric R. and MacKenzie, Donald W. 1976 'Donald Morrison' *Tocher* 24, 289-319.

Cregeen, Eric R. 1978 'Oral History in Scotland', a report of the conference of March 1978, *Oral History* Vol. 6, No. 2, 19—22.

Cregeen, Eric R. and Mackay, Margaret A. 1979 'Hector Kennedy' *Tocher* 32, 69–106.

Cregeen, Eric R. 1979 'The Changing Role of the House of Argyll in the Scottish Highlands' in Phillipson, N. T. and Mitchison, Rosalind (eds.) *Scotland in the Age of Improvement,* Edinburgh: Edinburgh University Press. 5-23. (Reprint 1996)

Cregeen, Eric R. 1979 'Tradition and Change in the West Highlands of Scotland' in Dyrvik, S., Mykland, K. and Oldervoll, J. (eds.) *The Satellite State in the 17th and 18th centuries,* Bergen, Oslo, Tromsø: Universitetsforlarget, 98-121.

Cregeen, Eric R. 1981 'Oral History', *Phonographic Bulletin* 29 (March) 9-14.

Cregeen, Eric R. 1981 'The Highlands since 1745', in Daiches, David (ed.) *A Companion to Scottish Culture* 164 and *A New Companion to Scottish Culture,* Edinburgh: Polygon, 1993, 140—42.

Cregeen, Eric R. 1983/1998 'Oral Tradition and History in a Hebridean Island' *Scottish Studies,* No. 32: 1993–98, (posthumously published 1998) 12-37.

Cregeen, Eric R. 1985 Preface in Nancy C Dorian, *The Tyranny of Tide: An Oral History of East Sutherland Fisherfolk,* Ann Arbor, pp. ix—xiii.

DOCUMENTARY FILM

'The Clearances' 1980 Scottish Television (STV), Script by Eric Cregeen and Patrick Boyle, narrated by Fulton Mackay and produced and directed by Patrick Boyle.

APPENDIX C

Publications about and including the work of Eric R. Cregeen

BOOKS

Cregeen, Eric R. and Bennett, Margaret (ed.) 2004 Foreword by Prof. T. C. Smout, Introduction by Margaret Bennett. *"Recollections of an Argyllshire Drover" & Other West Highland Chronicles by Eric R. Cregeen,* Edinburgh: Birlinn. Second edition, 2013, Crieff: Grace Note Publications.

Cregeen, Eric R. and Martin, Angus. 2011 *Kintyre Instructions: The 5th Duke of Argyll's Instructions to His Kintyre Chamberlain, 1785-1805*, Edinburgh: The Grimsay Press.

ARTICLES

Bennett, Margaret. 2009 'The Growth of the Oral History Movement in Scotland: The Life and Legacy of Eric R. Cregeen', *Oral History,* Vol. 37, No. 1, FORTY YEARS 1969-2009, 43-51.

Mackay, Margaret A. 2014 'From Machair to Prairie: Emigration from Tiree to Canada in the 19th and early 20th Centuries'. *The Secret Island: Towards a History of Tiree,* Kershader: Islands Book Trust: 170-197.

Mackay, Margaret A. 1996 (orig. publ. 1980). 'Poets and Pioneers' in *The Complete Odyssey: Voices from Scotland's Recent Past,* ed. Billy Kay. Edinburgh: Polygon, 58-69.

Mackay, Margaret A. and Meek, Donald E. (eds). 2016 "Sguaban a Tìr an Eòrna: Traditions of Tiree", Scottish Tradition CDTRAX9027, Greentrax Recordings Ltd.

Martin, Angus. 2001 'The MacKeith Family at Kilmichael' in *Kintyre Antiquarian and Natural History Magazine* No. 50, pp. 28-31. (Eric R. Cregeen›s field-notes of a visit to Kilmichael Farm, Carradale, on August 1, 1967.)

Scottish Studies: In memory of Eric Radcliffe Cregeen, 1921–1983, Vol. 32, 1993 to 98. The University of Edinburgh: Tuckwell Press.

The Secret Island: Towards a History of Tiree, 2014 (Throughout contributions to the book, which is the proceedings from a three-day conference, 2013, on Tiree), Kershader: Islands Book Trust.

Tindley A. (ed.) and Cregeen E. R. 2014 'A West Highland Census of 1779: social and economic trends on the Argyll Estate.' *Northern Scotland,* 5 (1), 75-105. Edinburgh: Edinburgh University Press.

Tindley A. (ed.) and Cregeen E.R. 2015 'The creation of the crofting townships in Tiree'. *Journal of Scottish Historical Studies*, 35(2), 155-188. Edinburgh: Edinburgh University Press.

DOCUMENTARY FILM

'Eric R. Cregeen – Thachair Sruth ri Steall (Eric R. Cregeen & the Carrying Stream)' 2019 MacTV, Stornoway for BBC Alba, narrated by Paraig Morrison, produced and directed by Niall Campbell.

ACKNOWLEDGEMENTS

We would like to thank all who transcribed the journals and also those (named and unnamed) who helped decipher the more challenging pages: Dr. Ann Petrie (Crieff), Archie Campbell (Benbecula); Brìd McKibbon (Inverness); Catherine (Irene) Fleming (Isle of Arran); David Cregeen Lawrence (Auchterarder); Deirdre McMahon (Edinburgh); Joan MacKenzie (Edinburgh); Julie Lewis (South Uist); Lynsey Sinclair (Isle of Skye); Pam MacKinnon (Edinburgh); Michelle Melville (Ballachulish) and Nicola Don (née Cregeen, Duns).

Though the completion of the transcriptions and printing of the journals marked the end of the original project, it was soon apparent that an index would be an essential tool for research. Massively time-consuming and demanding, the daunting task was undertaken by Dr Gonzalo J. Mazzei. As editor, I accept responsibility for classification of subjects and decisions on organisation of the content. All who access the journals will undoubtedly share my indebtedness and appreciation of Gonzalo's time, expertise and generosity, without which this index would not have appeared.

We are extremely grateful to Dr Michael Bauer (www.iGàidhlig.net) for helping to correct some of the errors in Gaelic transcriptions. They appear on an errata sheet inserted in relevant journals and will be corrected in the second print-run and on a dedicated web-page.

Finally, I would like to thank Ros and Russell Salton for the support they have given during the project and for helping to sustain my efforts to complete the 'last mile'.

Margaret Bennett